many garments, but all
fashioned from the
same designer

(me) wonder about the
use of words like
normative, rabbinic
(w) interpretation
in the final as hermeneutic
analysis / cut from one
cloth

THE GARMENTS
OF TORAH

Indiana Studies in Biblical Literature

Herbert Marks and Robert Polzin,
General Editors

THE GARMENTS
OF TORAH

Essays in
Biblical Hermeneutics

MICHAEL
FISHBANE

INDIANA UNIVERSITY PRESS
BLOOMINGTON & INDIANAPOLIS

Manufactured in the United States of America

Library of Congress Cataloging-in-Publication Data

Fishbane, Michael A.
The garments of torah: Essays in biblical
hermeneutics.

(Indiana studies in biblical literature)
Bibliography: p.
Includes index.
1. Bible. O.T.—Criticism, interpretation, etc.,
Jewish—History. 2. Bible. OT.—Hermeneutics.
I. Title. II. Series.
BS1186.F58   1989   221.6′01   88-46039
ISBN 0-253-32217-0
1 2 3 4 5 93 92 91 90 89

For EITAN

CONTENTS

PREFACE

Rereading these essays on biblical hermeneutics, written over the past decade and more, the polymorphous image of Hermes came repeatedly to mind. As a resourceful messenger, Hermes is, of course, the patron of hermeneutics itself. But he is also a numen of boundaries, an agent of monetary exchange, and even a frequent visitor to the netherworld of the dead. Many of these multiple aspects are recursively present in his hermeneutical guise, as well; or at least this is what attracts me to this figure, and to the hermeneutical process itself. For it seems to me that Hermes is the complex representation of a creative force by which we shuttle from our living present to the past, crossing the boundaries of time in order to revive bygone texts along with ourselves, their readers. Hermes is the coin of exchange whereby older texts and latter-day readers are reciprocally re-formed in each other's image. The prolongation of the life of a text, through exegesis, is thus also a process of symbolic immortality. For in text cultures the umbilical cord of hermeneutics is at once a life line to one's matrix in the past and a death-defying act of the imagination in the present. Scheherazade knew this secret well: if we reinvent the story forever, we may continue to live.

The three parts of this book reflect three typical moments whereby cultures renew themselves hermeneutically. Part I gives examples of the development of the exegetical imagination in Judaism, beginning with the Bible itself, and the changing images of Scripture that result. Part II traces two instances whereby exegetical choices and attitudes have shaped ancient biblical and rabbinic culture. The transformative praxis of interpretation is revealed here under the sign of its historical impact. The way we reformulate our historicity through the praxis of scholarly inquiry cannot be evaded, and one must therefore be ready to acknowledge that it is in and through the act of historical exegesis that we continuously rewrite our "myth of origins"—now in the form of historical or cultural commentaries. With this in mind, but especially mindful of the way ancient texts are exchanged for present realities, Part III explores several instances of the act of *Vergegenwärtigung*—of making the pastness of texts present to us and part of our ongoing cultural lives. In the powerful image of Franz Rosenzweig, when we read truly, we truly read texts like Scripture for their inner power (*innere Kraft*). Of the making of commentaries, then, there may be no end if we are to survive as a culture empowered by our historical past and the dynamic dimensions of its retrieval. The attentive reader will no doubt sense these different dialectics in the chapters at hand—not least the shifting boundaries of text and person, of author and authority, of word and will.

In sifting among my writings for examples which might make aspects of these issues accessible to the nonspecialist reader in some of their historical variety, I have also tried to choose essays which were delivered in public settings at one point or another. And as the topics discussed were often called forth by a communal or academic concern, I have tried to retain here something of the living voice with which I originally responded. I have indicated in the notes my thanks to the several publishers who have kindly granted permission to reprint these essays. To lighten the burden on the general reader, the more academic underpinnings of certain arguments have either been deleted or put in the notes, and the system of transliterating Hebrew words has been highly simplified. I have also tended to separate conjunctions, prepositions and definite articles from the words cited, so that the common form commented on in several places will be obvious to the non-Hebraist. As a further concession in this direction, I have regularly presented certain consonants in their voiceless form even where they were pronounced otherwise (e.g., 'b' for 'v'). This, too, was done to highlight word patterns in a text. The only exceptions are several person names or book titles which by now have a conventional spelling in the English-speaking world.

I am grateful to the editorial staff of Indiana University Press for understanding this matter. I am also thankful to the Press for its many courtesies, and for the professional manner with which they have produced this book. Their interest in these essays was a wonderful spur to gather them in this form. In this regard, I also wish to thank the editors of the Indiana Studies in Biblical Literature for their interest—particularly Herbert Marks, whose comments were always thoughtful and insightful.

As the earliest of these essays was written in Jerusalem in 1975, just before my oldest son Eitan was born, and now these words are also written in Jerusalem just weeks before his becoming a Bar Mitzvah, it gives me the deepest pleasure to dedicate this book to him in love and respect. As his name is a symbol in Jewish mystical texts for the highest key of interpretation, it is my prayer that his imagination and compassion, already so evident, never fail him as he comes before the ever-changing gates of mystery.

Michael Fishbane
Institute for Advanced Studies
Hebrew University
November, 1988

·I·

THE HERMENEUTICS OF
SCRIPTURE IN FORMATION

· 1 ·

INNER-BIBLICAL EXEGESIS: TYPES AND STRATEGIES OF INTERPRETATION IN ANCIENT ISRAEL

One of the great and most characteristic features of the history of religions is the ongoing reinterpretation of sacred utterances which are believed to be foundational for each culture. So deeply has this phenomenon become part of our modern literary inheritance that we may overlook the peculiar type of imagination which it has sponsored and continues to nurture: an imagination which responds to and is deeply dependent upon received traditions; an imagination whose creativity is never entirely a new creation, but one founded upon older and authoritative words and images. This paradoxical dynamic, whereby religious change is characterized more often by revisions and explications of a traditional content than by new visions or abrupt innovations, is strikingly demonstrated by the fate of the teachings of Gautama Buddha. For if this remarkable teacher devoted himself to the ideal of breaking free of tradition and the dependencies thereby engendered, his disciples quickly turned his own words into sutras for commentary. Among the great western religions, however, Judaism has sought to dignify the status of religious commentary, and in one popular mythic image transferred to it a metaphysical dimension. For the well-known Talmudic image of God studying and interpreting his own Torah is nothing if not that tradition's realization that there is no authoritative teaching which is not also the source of its own renewal, that revealed teachings are a dead letter unless revitalized in the mouth of those who study them.[1]

Pharisaic Judaism tried to minimize the gap between a divine Torah and ongoing human interpretation by projecting the origins of authorita-

Originally published in *Midrash and Literature*, ed. G. H. Hartman and S. Budick (New Haven, Conn.: Yale University Press, 1986) and reprinted by permission.

tive exegesis to Sinai itself.[2] But even this mythification of a chain of legitimate interpreters did not so much obscure the distinction between Revelation and Interpretation as underscore it. From this perspective, the interpretative traditions of ancient Judaism constitute a separate, non-biblical genre: a post-biblical corpus of texts which stand alongside the Sinaitic Revelation as *revelation* of new meanings *through exegesis*. Moreover, this dignification of interpretation in Pharisaic literature highlights another feature of ancient Judaism (and is a root cause of early Jewish polemics): the realization that there was no pure teaching of Revelation apart from its regeneration or clarification through an authoritative type of exegesis. The rabbinic guardians of Torah claimed to be its true teachers, their oral exegesis the only valid password to the written text.

Given these two issues—the distinction between Revelation and interpretative tradition, and their complex interdependence—we may ask: Do we in fact cross a great divide from the Hebrew Bible to its rabbinic interpreters, or is the foundation text *already* an interpreted document—despite all initial impressions to the contrary? Certainly any divide that may be perceived becomes a slippery slope when we look at the era around 150 B.C.E., which saw 1) the end to the production of texts which would be given authority in the canon of the Hebrew Bible and, 2) a proliferation of many and sophisticated modes of exegesis, in the legal and prophetic documents of the Qumran sectaries, in the rewritten biblical histories composed by proto- and para-Pharisaic circles (such as the *Book of Jubilees* or the *Testaments of the Twelve Patriarchs*), and in the Bible versions of the Greek-speaking Jews of Alexandria or the Samaritan community near Mt. Gerizim. To say, then, that rabbinic exegesis was fundamentally dependent upon trends in contemporary Greco-Roman rhetoric or among the Alexandrian grammarians is to mistake ecumenical currents of text-study and the occurrence of similar exegetical terms for the inner-Jewish cultivation of preexistent native traditions of interpretation.[3]

In what follows we shall explore some of the types of textual interpretation in ancient Israel—that is, within the Hebrew Bible itself—paying particular attention to how the texts that comprise it were revised and even reauthorized during the course of many centuries, and to how older traditions fostered new insights which, in turn, thickened the intertextual matrix of the culture and conditioned its imagination. Without any attempt to be comprehensive, we hope to suggest some of the ways by which the foundation document of Judaism, the Hebrew Bible, not only sponsored a monumental culture of textual exegesis but was itself its own first product. We shall first consider the area of scribal exegesis and follow this with more extensive considerations of both legal exegesis and strategic revision in the Hebrew Bible.[4]

I

The process of the intercultural transmission of traditions may be considered one of the primary areas in which authoritative teachings or memories were received and revalued for new generations. Ancient Near Eastern myths were theologically adapted and historicized; nomadic recollections were revised in order to promote the prestige and claims of tribal ancestors; and narrative topoi were reworked with new moral or theological considerations in mind.[5] As the ancient oral culture was subsumed into a developing text culture by the first millennium B.C.E., these processes continued but were often more narrowly circumscribed. Then also, as before, the culture determined its values by what it chose to receive and transmit as authoritative. However, revision of these materials was increasingly more affected by the discriminating eye of the trained scribe, as he patiently copied out a text and reacted to its ambiguities and oddities, than by the ear of the wise cognoscenti of the tribe. Thus we find numerous instances in which old toponyms are retained but supplemented by their newer name ("Luz: it is Bethel"; Josh. 18:13), or foreign terms are translated on the spot ("pur: it is the lot"; Esther 3:7). As often as not these explanatory glosses are introduced by formulaic terms, thus underscoring the professional background of the scribal insertions. Moreover, even by such meager evidence, it is clear that the authoritative text being explicated was not considered inviolable but subject to the invasion of a tradition of interpretation which rendered it more comprehensible.

Such scribal intrusions should not be minimized, for they open a valuable window upon the regard ancient Israelite scribes had for authoritative texts, whose obliquities were retained alongside their explication. Indeed, it would certainly have been easier and more economical for these scribes to have removed or reformulated the disturbing words. For example, the scribes who noticed the jarring oddity in the historical narrative of Ezra 3:12 (which reports that when the cornerstone of the post-exilic second Temple was laid, "many priests, Levites, heads of patriarchal clans, and elders who had seen this first Temple *when it was founded* . . . cried loudly"), could have simply deleted the clause "when it was founded" or rephrased it so as to specify the ambiguous pronoun "it." For, as the text now stands, "it" may refer either to the founding of the contemporary second Temple or to the founding of the first one, four hundred years earlier—a historical howler. However, to resolve this ambiguity, the explicator chose neither of the aforenoted alternatives but inserted the syntactically disruptive phrase *"this is [refers to] the Temple"* after the words "when it was founded." Such a phrase manifestly directs the reader to the proper historical sense of the phrase; namely, a reference to the founding of the second Temple.[6] The point, then, is that "many priests," etc., who had seen the first Temple in its glory were dismayed and cried when they observed the foundation of the more modest second one. But since the explicatory comment pokes disruptingly out of the sentence, the latter-day reader is still constrained to pause and notice the original reading. Paradoxically then, by retaining the old together with the new, the scribes have insured that future readers would be forced to a realization not far removed from their own: that they are latecomers to the text, who must read it with the guidance of an oral—now written—exegetical tradition.

Such processes become all the more intriguing in texts which lay an even higher claim upon the culture: texts which claim to be divine revelations. Isa. 29:9–11 provides an instructive case.

9. Be astonished and dazed, revel and be blinded: you have drunk, but not from wine; totter, but not from drink;

10. For YHWH has poured over you a spirit of stupefaction: He has closed your eyes—*namely, the prophets*—and cloaked your heads—*the seers;*

11. All prophetic visions shall be sealed from you . . .

The object of the denunciation beginning in v. 9 is unspecified. But inasmuch as the people of Judaea have been the object of scorn throughout the preceding oracles, and no new subject has been introduced, one may reasonably infer that the reference is to the people. It is they who are drunk and totter and who cannot fathom the prophetic visions given to them. From this perspective, the words "namely, the prophets" and "the seers" are problematic and reflect a shift in subject from the people to the prophets. Moreover, since these two phrases have a syntactically distinct, appositional relationship to their preceding clauses (the first is actually introduced by the particle *'et,*[7] which normally introduces a direct object, *after* a clause ending with an object), and since the clauses without these disruptive words actually form a coherent chiasmus (literally, "He has closed your eyes" is inversely parallel to "your heads He has cloaked"), it is likely that Isa. 29:10 preserves scribal explications intruded into the old oracle.[8] A motivating concern of these interpretative comments may have been to elucidate the literary figure of "closed eyes." The result, however, is that an oracle condemning the people is transformed into a rebuke of false prophets. Tendentious motivations cannot, therefore, be entirely excluded. But whatever their origin or aim, the scribal comments in v. 10 were made relatively early, for the Septuagint version presupposes the problematic syntax now found in the received Massoretic text and tries to normalize the prophetic condemnation—while extending its scope yet further.[9] The Lucianic reviser of this Greek text has further compounded the tissue of errors by seeking to improve on the Septuagint version which he had himself inherited without (apparently) ever consulting the Massoretic Hebrew version which we have cited.[10]

From the viewpoint of the exegetical process involved, the textual strata represented by the Massoretic text and by the Septuagint and its Lucianic recension reflect continuous rereadings of the original oracle, though it is clear that the scribal hand which inserted "namely, the prophets" and "the seers" into Isa. 29:10 reflects the most invasive exegetical procedure, which transforms the meaning of the passage and disturbs its syntactic balance—a matter the later translators-commentators tried to rectify. Moreover, this striking transformation of an oracle against the people into one against the prophets shows the extent to which the interpretative tradition (we do not know if the scribe reflects his own reading or mediates that of a school) might introduce a new authority into a received tradition, so that these *human* comments compete with and ultimately transform the focus of the ancient, *divine* words. Accordingly, Isa. 29:9–11 succinctly underscores a paradoxical dimension of scribal exegesis; namely, that the tradition it receives (in this case, an oracle) is not necessarily the one it transmits. For the latter is now the bearer of multiple authorities for that generation of readers: the privileged voice of divine Revelation and the human voice of instruction have become one. That this paradox is not always perceived is a measure of the scribes' success in subordinating their voice to that of the tradition. Even more paradoxically: in the end it is *their* interpretations that have become the received tradition; their oral traditions are the written text given to the community.

II

We began our discussion of interpretation in ancient Israel by considering some aspects of scribal exegesis. These concisely demonstrate the dynamics which also characterize legal and theological exegesis. For if scribalism points to the fact that ordinary textual ambiguity or openness may serve to catalyze commentary and that these supplements, when incorporated into the received text, reflect the cultural dynamics of transmission, then law and theology, where the frequent incomprehensibility or noncomprehensiveness of divinely authorized rules requires human exegesis and expansion, offer an even richer sphere for study.[11]

At the outset, let us consider a case where the borders between scribal exegesis and legal instruction are somewhat blurred. Like the example in Isa. 29:9–11, here again we have a skein of successive explications, though now embedded entirely within the Hebrew text. Thus Lev. 19:19 provides a rule prohibiting different forms of mixtures: the mixed breeding of cattle, the mixture of sown seeds in a field, and the mixture of textiles in a garment. The injunction is formulaic and repeats the key-term *kilayim*, "mixtures." One may easily assume that the precise application of the general categories *cattle* and *field* were known to the audience or supplemented by oral tradition, so that the rule could be properly obeyed; and, indeed, when this teaching is repeated in Deut. 22:9–11 as Moses' own, one finds that the meaning of the legal topos of *field* in this rule is in fact unfolded in several directions (v. 9).[12] It is, however, to the rule prohibiting textile mixtures that special notice may be given here: for the spare and rhythmic phraseology in the priestly rule is in this one instance disrupted by a pleonastic word, *shaʿatnez*, which is in asyndetic opposition to *kilayim* and clearly intended to explain it. Whether this addition is a scribal comment or the written articulation of an oral tradition, it is certain that the intrusive *shaʿatnez* constituted no lexical difficulty—which it clearly did in the later deuteronomic revision of the rule, where *kilayim* is deleted and the explicatory remark "wool and flax" is now in asyndetic opposition to *shaʿatnez*.

Given the expository, often revisionary nature of many deuteronomic repetitions of earlier rules, one may conclude that in this particular instance the interpretative tradition has broken into the text and established itself as the written, revealed teaching of God to Moses. Conceivably, it was believed that the instructive elaboration only made explicit what the traditional rule meant all along and that there was no intent to displace the authoritative divine voice, even though this was itself doubly mediated through Moses' revision of the original revelation. Nevertheless, the jostling of successive cultural voices in this skein of pentateuchal texts, and the convergence of human instruction with divine Revelation so that the former partakes of the prestige of the latter but also makes it viable, demonstrates a root feature and the paradoxical task of inner-biblical (as well as later Jewish) exegesis: to extend the divine voice into historical time while reasserting and reestablishing its hierarchical preeminence over all other cultural voices.

Such a task for legal exegesis is the ideal, of course; and it is largely achieved in the Hebrew Bible as we have it, though often as the result of textual finesse. A valiant tour de force in this regard occurs in a series of exegetical revisions of the sabbatical legislation in Exod. 23:10–11, made in order to insure its comprehensiveness and interpretability. In vv. 10–11a the old rule states, "You shall sow your land for six years and reap its yield, but [during] the seventh you shall let it lie fallow and abandon it; let the poor of your nation eat thereof, and let the beast of the field eat what they leave over." This stipulation is clearly limited to sown fields (agriculture). But as this would hardly have proved comprehensive in ancient Israel, the divine rule is supplemented in v. 11b by an analogical extension that includes vineyards and olive groves (viticulture), "*You shall do likewise to your vineyard and your olive grove.*" This addendum is introduced by a technical formula (*ken ta'aseh*) frequently used for such purposes in biblical regulations.[13] But even this extension and absorption of a human supplement into a rule with divine authority was hardly the end of the matter: for the manner of application is left unstated. Could one prune in the seventh year, though not reap? or eat from the vine if one did not prune it?

Undoubtedly these and similar ambiguities were resolved by oral exegesis, and so it is quite notable when this appears in a written form, as in the repetition of a rule in Lev. 25:3–7, which dutifully takes up each of the operative phrases in Exod. 23:10–11a and clarifies every point in vv. 4–7 in the light of questions that had emerged in lawyerly and popular circles. For example, to the original lemma concerning the sabbatical release of sown fields and vineyards it adds: "you shall not sow your field or prune your vineyard; you shall not reap the aftergrowth of your harvest or gather the grapes of your untrimmed vines." But the most striking feature of this legal explication, which is not presented as a Mosaic repetition of an earlier dictum but as an original divine prescription, is the way it obscures innovation by its syntactical incorporation of the addendum of Exod. 23:11b into its citation of v. 10 ("You shall sow your fields for six years—*and you shall prune your vineyard for six years*—and reap its yield"). Quite clearly the emphasized clause is syntactically awkward and partially redundant, but the result is quite significant, for the original addendum has been normalized and with it the technical formula "you shall do likewise" dropped. In the process, the interpretative voice has been obscured, or redignified as a divine voice. Indeed, it is largely by means of such intrusions of living legal commentary into preexistent written rules that we can to some extent monitor the dependence of the divine teachings upon their human articulation in ancient Israel and the corresponding drive for pseudepigraphic anonymity in legal exegesis. But piety aside, what interpreter could ever hope for a better "hearing" for his words than by this self-effacement, by this covertly promethean act?

Rarely does the human teacher forget and starkly betray himself in his cultural task; though one may admit that he does so in Num. 15:22–29, when, prior to a phrase-by-phrase elaboration of Lev. 4:13–21, 27–31 (e.g., compare Lev. 4:20b with Num. 15:25–26), the comment is made that the ensuing teachings are those "which YHWH spoke to Moses" (v. 22; cf. v. 23)—even though the framework of the instructions is YHWH's active command to Moses to speak the divine words to the people. Thus the teacher has doubled (and, in a sense, subverted) the levels of authority in the text by revealing that his instruction quietly extends Moses' original recitation of the divine words. Jeremiah, on the other hand, in a later expansion of the Sabbath rule in the Decalogue (Deut. 5:12–13), more deftly obscures his handiwork. This maneuver deserves some comment.

The terse formulation prohibiting Sabbath labor found in the Decalogue, Exod. 20:18–21, is taken over virtually verbatim in the Mosaic citation of it in Deut. 5:12–14: "Heed the Sabbath day to sanctify it—as YHWH, your God, commanded you. Six days you may labor and do all your work, but the seventh is the Sabbath of YHWH, your God: do not do any work." But even Moses' recitation of the ancient rule ("as YHWH . . . commanded you") does little to explicate the details of prohibited work—a feature which was undoubtedly clarified by the oral and interpretative tradition, and which was part of the ongoing teaching of the priests whose mandate was "to instruct the Israelites" that they separate "the sacred from the profane" (Lev. 10:10–11; cf. Mal. 2:4–7). In this respect, it is significant to note that injunctions whose language is extremely similar to that of the Decalogue in Exodus are subsequently recited with such notable additions as that one who works "will be put to death" (see Exod. 31:12–18, esp. vv. 14–15), or that the definition of prohibited work included igniting fires (Exod. 35:1–3) or ignoring Sabbath rest during peak harvest seasons (Exod. 34:21). The ongoing process of legal clarification is also evident in narratives which report divine prohibitions of food-gathering (and baking or boiling foods) or wood-gathering on the Sabbath day (Exod. 16:4–27; Num. 15:32–36); and it seems that travels for mercenary purposes or even business negotiations were strongly discouraged in later periods (Isa. 58:13).

Jer. 17:21–22 falls within this larger compass of exegetical addenda to Sabbath rules. The notable difference from earlier types of revision of the Decalogue is that this one occurs within a prophetic oracle, not in a legal or priestly teaching. Its outward form is that of Jeremiah reporting God's command to address the people at one of the central gates of Jerusalem (vv. 19–20), and then his presentation of the oracle (vv. 21–27) in the divine voice (first person)—after an introit which disclaims his own authority: "Thus says YHWH: Be heedful *and do not bear any burden [for commerce]*[14] *on the Sabbath day and bring it to the gates of Jerusalem; and do not take any burden from your homes on the Sabbath day.* Do not do any work: you shall sanctify the Sabbath day, as I commanded *your forefathers*" (vv. 21–22). A close comparison of this citation with the passage from Deut. 5:12–14 cited earlier shows that such phrases as "be heedful," "the Sabbath day," "do not do any work," "you shall sanctify the Sabbath day," and "I commanded" are directly derived from that version of the Decalogue; whereas the emphasized clauses, which are embedded within this pentateuchal citation, explicate the rules of prohibited Sabbath labor by doubly restricting them: first, by prohibiting the bearing of burdens from one's house to the gates of Jerusalem for storage or sale;[15] and, second, by prohibiting the transfer of burdens from the private to the public domain. The fact that this second prohibition so circumscribes the first as virtually to obviate it, and that it is also not mentioned in vv. 24–27, whereas the first prohibition is, may suggest that this clause restricting bearable goods to one's home on the Sabbath is a secondary addition to the oracle—much as the Septuagint inserted the post-biblical prohibition of extended Sabbath travel into its own recension of v. 21 ("and do not go out of the gates of Jerusalem").

In any event, it is not solely the oracle-form, which uses the Decalogue as the framework for its exegetical expansions, that arrests one's attention. The more remarkable fact is that the divine voice adverts to the deuteronomic text ("as I commanded your forefathers") as if to emphasize the antiquity of the prohibition. For, by this means, the divine voice speaking through Jeremiah does not just reinforce the prohibition or merely cite Deut. 5:12 ("as YHWH . . . commanded you") but *uses* this quotation-tag to authorize the legal innovation and imply that the Sabbath rule now articulated—with its additions—is the very same that was taught at Sinai! The new teachings are authorized by a pseudo-citation from the Pentateuch, spoken with divine authority.

This revision of the Mosaic recitation of an earlier divine command is thus an exemplary case of the exegetical extensions some legal teachings underwent in biblical literature. They preserve the hierarchical preeminence of the divine voice at all costs. But by the very activation of the earlier source via its citation, the hermeneutical imagination at work in Jer. 17:21–22 betrays itself: its desire to prolong the divine voice into a present which presupposes the entire Sinaitic revelation, and its willingness to subordinate the human exegetical voice, whose undisguised presence would then underscore a gap in the authority of the revealed law. The paradox of the interrelatedness and interdependence of revealed Torah and interpretative tradition is, it seems to me, no more firmly expressed and repressed than in this remarkable case of inner-biblical exegesis found in the ancient Book of Jeremiah.

III

We may turn again to the oracles of Jeremiah in order to appreciate another aspect of the exegetical process found in the Hebrew Bible, one which expresses new teachings by means of strategic revisions of earlier traditions, often from different genres. Indeed, these reappropriations and transformations indicate the extent to which older authorities were in the mind of later teachers and part of their imagination—suggestively radicalizing their rhetorical stance through allusions to, and departures from, inherited *logia*. Many and varied are the forms of this achievement, whose range extends from discourses and oracles on the one hand to liturgies and historiography on the other.[16] In the process, many old revelations or traditions come alive.

Our appreciation of the oracle in Jer. 2:3 can be enhanced by a detour through another series of exegetical transformations: those which link and divide Exod. 19:5–6 from Deut. 7:6. In the deuteronomic revision of its source we find articulated a theological characterization of Israel which is presupposed by the divine oracle expressed by Jeremiah. Significantly, the first text from Exod. 19:5–6 is cast as a revelation through Moses— before the Sinaitic revelation—that informs the people "if you heed My voice and observe My covenant then you will be My special possession among the nations . . . and My . . . holy [*qadosh*] nation." Quite evidently the holy status of Israel is portrayed here as contingent on covenantal obedience. Given this, Moses' later independent recitation of this speech is remarkable for its transformation of Israel's status as unqualifiedly and unconditionally holy: "For you are a holy [*qadosh*] people to YHWH, your God . . . [His] special people among the nations." No longer is Israel's holiness a condition dependent upon covenantal obedience. It is now the preeminent condition for Israel's obedience to the divine regulations, such as those mentioned in vv. 1–5. With this in mind, as perhaps it was in the mind of the audience that once heard Jeremiah's oration, we may turn to the oracle itself: "Israel is consecrated [*qodesh*] to YHWH, the first fruits of His produce; whoever destroys him [*okhelav*] will be judged guilty [*ye'eshamu*], and evil will befall them: oracle of YHWH."

One detects here a slight discrepancy between the reference to YHWH at the outset of the oracle and the closing formula which often denotes direct speech. Either Jeremiah or his disciples obscured the authority of the *prophetic* voice by the higher authority of the divine voice speaking directly. It is also conceivable that the final quotation mark serves to indicate that the prophet spoke about God under divine inspiration and was not of himself speaking divine words. At any rate, this initial mote that sticks in our eye, suggesting a tension between tradition and innovation, enlarges to a beam as the reference to Israel's special holiness recalls the tradition found in Moses' deuteronomic speech, and we observe the new setting and imagery which has renovated it. The more complicated intertextuality of the Jeremiah oracle stands revealed, and with it a remarkable instance of exegetical revision. To be sure, we cannot gauge exactly what was known by Jeremiah's audience, but we may safely say that the prophet is utilizing the following technical piece of priestly legislation:

And if a man eats a consecrated [*qodesh*] donation by accident, he must add one-fifth to its value and give the consecrated item to the priest. And they [the priests] shall not allow the consecrated donation of the Israelites to be desecrated, and thereby cause them [the Israelites] to bear [their] iniquity[17] of guilt [*ashmah*] when they [the Israelites] eat [*okhelam*] their [own] consecrated donations . . .

This regulation deals with the accidental desacralization by the laity of consecrated offerings donated to the Lord for the priests. The priests are to be vigilant in this: not for their own self-interest—since they nevertheless receive the perquisite plus a penalty surcharge in case of its desecration—but for the laity's sake, for through such inadvertence they cause the people to incur guilt. And because the regulation in Lev. 22:14–16 refers to concrete cultic behavior, the terms used have concrete force: the "consecrated" donations refer specifically to those animals and products (including first fruits) mentioned in Num. 18:11–19, 25–29, especially v. 12; the "eating" thereof means just that; and the "guilt" incurred involves a fixed reparation. Not so Jer. 2:3, which clearly uses all these technical terms but transforms them in an idiosyncratic, exegetical way. Indeed, in Jeremiah's rhetoric the various terms take on a figurative, even metaphorical, aspect. Israel, the covenant people, is not only "consecrated" to the Lord but His own "first fruits"; the "eating" thereof is semantically extended to connote destruction;[18] and the "guilt" involved is not a cultic fault requiring reparation but a matter of historical accountability.

The semantic transformations in this passage thus conceal a series of analogies with the older ritual rule. Israel is the consecrated donation of YHWH, just as the cultic offerings are the consecrated donations of the lay Israelites; and Israel's destruction by enemies involves retaliatory punishments, just as the accidental desecration of donations requires retributive reparation. But of course the analogies are not all symmetrical either—and this divergence gives hermeneutical power and tension to the new declaration. While the priestly rule is concerned with ritual accidents, Jeremiah's words imply aggressive intent; while the ritual accident in the priestly rule is committed by the donor, the destruction of Israel (the "ritual object") in the prophetic oracle is by a third party; while the reparation for the cultic fault is paid by the donor to the donee, in Jeremiah's reinterpretation of it the possessor (YHWH) of the holy produce (Israel) punishes those (the nations) who desecrate it.

These various asymmetries do not subvert the rhetorical force and analogical power of the exegetical application. Indeed, the evocation of an earlier textual authority through the diction and topos chosen for this new prophetic oracle so reactivates the older language as to provide a semantic foil for its revision. A simultaneity of voices is heard—the divine voice speaking the priestly rule through Moses, and the divine voice which uses its own words as it speaks through Jeremiah—and they do not cancel each other out.

But just what is it that generates Jeremiah's exegetical revival and reapplication of a relatively obscure priestly rule? We may return to the beginning of our discussion and suggest that the reason probably lies in, and may even draw upon, the same reinterpretation of the status of Israel as "holy," reflected in the deuteronomic revision of Exod. 19:4–6 noted earlier. The topos of Israel's sanctity and covenantal guilt may have activated old priestly associations and produced an oracle that gave cultic concreteness to the notion of Israel as a holy people. In a comparable way the deuteronomic draftsman has thoroughly transformed the conditional notion of Israel being a "priestly nation" found in Exod. 19:6 when he revised in Deut. 14:1–2 a rule from Lev. 21:5–6 which prohibited priests, consecrated to holiness, to cut their skin or pull out their hair when in mourning. In the deuteronomic text the *entire* people is categorically prohibited from doing this, precisely because it is, unconditionally, "a holy nation to YHWH."

The exegetical redeployment of Lev. 22:14–16 as a metonym for all the covenantal laws may serve as a concrete instance of the strategic re-employment of one delimited textual unit within another, equally delimited one. It is one type of the *textual-exegetical thinking* found in the Hebrew Bible. A related but distinct type is found where a later voice (real or fictive) speaks to a new situation by means of a variety of textual units, which are severally activated and in some instances transformed in their new setting.

As an example, we may consider 2 Chron. 15:2–7, a speech in which one Azzariah ben Oded delivers an oracle to King Asa of Judah:

2. YHWH will be with you when you are with Him: for if you seek Him [*tidreshuhu*], He will be present [*yimatze*] to you; but if you abandon Him, He will abandon you.
3. Now for a long time Israel was without a true God, without an instructing priest and without Torah.
4. But when in distress [*batzar*] Israel turned [*vayashabv*] to YHWH, God of Israel, and sought Him [*vayebaqshuhu*], He was present [*vayimatze*] to them.
5. On those times there was no peace for those who went out or came in [from battle], for tremendous disturbances [*mehumot rabot*] assailed the inhabitants of the lands.
6. And nations and cities smashed each other to bits, for God confounded them with every distress.
7. But now: be you strong and do not slacken: for there is recompense for your deeds.

This prophetic discourse (as also the prophet in whose name it is spoken) is unknown to earlier biblical sources, and appears to reflect the pseudepigraphic handiwork of the Chronicler who has woven together several strands of tradition in order to confront his contemporary readership (in the Persian period) with a matter of "prophetic" concern to him. The piece opens and closes (vv. 2, 7) with echoes of exhortation known from earlier sources ("YHWH will be with you"; "be strong") where it introduces an attempt to press someone into military or even prophetic service. But the exhortation appears here with the assertion that YHWH will be present to those who seek Him and follow his ways, so that the old military language has been thoroughly subordinated, even transformed, by being juxtaposed to spiritual-covenantal concerns—much as the similar exhortation of strength in Deut. 31:7–8 is transfigured and reinterpreted as strength for spiritual endeavors in Josh. 1:7–8, which recites the earlier speech.

But the exegetical dimensions of this speech are more ramified. At first glance the resumption of v. 2 by vv. 3–6, which describes a time when YHWH abandoned Israel because of her sins but also anticipates a return of divine presence to sincere penitents, seems to be an indeterminate rhetorical conceit. But a closer inspection of the verses suggests that the Chronicler is actually alluding to the recent exile and reminding the people that repentance may reverse the terror of divine abandonment. A striking parallel occurs in Deut. 4:29–30, a passage also of post-exilic origin, where the Israelites are told that if they beseech (*ubiqkashtem*) and seek (*tidreshenu*) YHWH and repent (*veshabta*, "turn") in distress (*batzar*), He will be present to them (*umetza'ukha*).

To portray the physical and spiritual horrors of exile, the Chronicler surrounds v. 4 with passages from earlier oracles of doom. Thus the Chronicler's reference in v. 5b to "tremendous disturbances" (using the rare expression *mehumot rabot*) is based on Amos 3:17. And v. 3, "for a long time Israel was without a true God, without an instructing priest, and without Torah," is actually an exegetical revision of Hos. 3:4, which refers to the northern exile with the words "for many days the Israelites dwelt without a king . . . or slaughter[19] . . . or image [*ephod*] or household gods [*teraphim*]." Like this passage, the Chronicler has Azzariah refer to "many days" in exile "without a king" and without means of divine instruction. But instead of referring to the older mantic means of instruction known to Hosea, the later Chronicler is concerned to emphasize instruction by priests—though he may also allude to the loss of the priestly tradition of mantic practice in the exile (cf. Ezra 2:63). In any event, the Chronicler's striking revision of the Hosean text is underscored by his reference to "Torah"—a matter unnoted in Hos. 3:4 but of recurrent concern to later biblical historiography.[20] In the light of the impact this old oracle had on the Chronicler, it should not pass unnoticed that the prophet Hosea closes his list of losses with the comment: "After that the Israelites will turn [*yashubu*] and seek [*ubiqshu*] YHWH" (v. 5). The Chronicler does likewise.

Azzariah's speech not only reuses older phrases and recontextualizes them, but the very allusions of his speech evoke these older texts and draw lines of signification out from 2 Chron. 15:2–7 to the richer textual-traditionary mass which stands behind the latter-day exhortation. Indeed, each of the allusions is very much like a metonym for a different lemma in the tradition, so that the speaker in the Chronicler's text is a new-old voice: a voice of the present hour, but also a voice which verbalizes older language for the sake of the reappropriation of the tradition. The sub-stitutions or additions in the Chronicler's text take on added force from this point of view. For the ear which heard or the eye which read these words would presumably perceive in their difference from the older literary models the gap of historical time which had intervened between the one occasion and the other; but it would also, perhaps, have recog-nized the earnest concerns which generate the textual imagination here at play. In this exegetical anthology, as in others from the period, older textual boundaries collapse before the pressure of an appropriating voice, and the complex intertextuality of the culture is brought to view. Here, all significant speech is scriptural or scripturally-oriented speech. The voices of Israel's teachers will struggle to speak anew in traditions and words handed down from the past: Jacob and his exegetical imagination will always be a supplanter seeking the blessing of antiquity.

IV

This brief review of inner-biblical exegesis is hardly a comprehensive display of its achievement in ancient Israelite literature. It may neverthe-less serve to isolate some strains of this important phenomenon, and it may even suggest some strategies used for retrieving older lemmata centuries before the emergence of classical Judaism and its forms of biblical exegesis.

One of the features that emerges prominently is the fact that for inner-biblical exegesis there is no merely literary or theological playfulness. Exegesis arises out of a practical crisis of some sort—the incomprehen-sibility of a word or a rule, or the failure of the covenantal tradition to engage its audience. There is, then, something of the dynamic of "tradi-tion and the individual talent" here—where the tradition sets the agenda of problems which must be creatively resolved or determines the received language which may be imaginatively reworked. The strategies vary from textual annotation, literary allusion, and types of analogical or synthetic reasoning. They include also the ethical, legal or even spiritual transformation of textual content.[21] In all cases the "tradition" maintains its generative and often determinative hierarchical preeminence, even as "individual talent" (of an individual in fact, or a school representative) clarifies or transforms tradition in the light of present-day ignorance or other exigencies.

Almost invariably, moreover, in the evidence preserved, individual talent has persistently exploited the received traditional context. Thus there are virtually no generalizations, abstractions, or context-free comments of the kind one finds in the developed rationality of Roman and Rabbinic Law. By the same token, abstract rules for rhetoric or prophetic discourse are not given, nor are there collocations of similar rhetorical types as in both early and late rabbinic Midrash. Tradition is the warp and woof of creative talent, the textual content whose lexical or theological knots are exegetically unraveled, separated, or recombined. In this sense tradition is also the retextured con-text.

But, further, tradition is often presented or represented as revelation. And so, from the viewpoint of how a new teaching is authorized, the intriguing issue is not just the interdependence of the two (i.e., how a new teaching uses the tradition) but the strategic subordination of the one to the other—what we may consider under the general category of "revelation and the individual talent." Our biblical sources display a complex variety of types along a spectrum that only in part reflects historical development. In some cases, new post-Sinaitic legal revelations given to Moses add exegetical content which had emerged over time; and in other instances, exegetical addenda are interpolated into the Mosaic mediation of the divine voice (in the laws found in Exodus or Leviticus) or the double mediation of that voice (in Deuteronomy). In still other cases legal innovations are mediated through a later prophetic voice (in Jer. 17:21–22, which uses Jeremiah; or Ezek. 44:9–31, which uses Ezekiel) or introduce exegetical developments under the authoritative citation of the Torah of Moses (in Ezra 9) or more obliquely (in the complex extension of Num. 9:9–14 in 2 Chron. 30:2–3). Only in the latter cases does the exegete's voice emerge to full view—an event of real cultural consequence.

The strategic subordination of the human exegetical voice to divine revelation in the Hebrew Bible should not, however, be regarded as a case of pious fraud or political manipulation of older sources—though here and there this perspective cannot be excluded. Rather we should recognize the inevitable preeminence of the divine voice in biblical culture and realize that many legal additions, for example, made the law livable; so that an interpreter may well have often believed that his interpretation was the explicit articulation of the received content of the tradition and that individual talent was marked by its very ability to perform this feat. It even seems likely that some circles believed the legal exegetes were inspired by God to perform their task through the very study of the divine word.[22] But this is not certain. In any case, the existence of revealed texts in the mind of later prophets was certainly a catalytic factor in their production of remarkably innovative discourses. The example from Jer. 17:21–22 is not the only case in point, for one could well point to Malachi's striking reuse and inversion of the Priestly Blessing in Mal. 1:6–2:9 as an additional instance, among others.[23] The case of Azzariah ben Oded, furthermore, shows how Revelation may activate older traditions in our historiographical sources—although as a rule the individual talent of the historian is disguised in the oblique, but no less authoritative, voice of the historical narrator.

Whether aggressive or naive, fully self-conscious or the product of divine inspiration, textual exegeses in the Hebrew Bible oscillate between the authoritatively given lemma and its renovation through syntactic, semantic, or generic manoeuvers. One may say that the entire corpus of Scripture remains open to these invasive procedures and strategic reworkings up to the close of the canon in the early rabbinic period, and so the received text is complexly compacted of teachings and their subversion, of rules and their extension, of topoi and their revision. Within ancient Israel, as long as the textual corpus remained open, Revelation and Tradition were thickly interwoven and interdependent, and the received Hebrew Bible is itself, therefore, the product of an interpretative tradition.

With the closing of the corpus of Scripture, however, and the establishment of a fixed canon deemed prior in time and authority to rabbinic exegesis, there was a tendency to forget the exegetical dimensions of Scripture and to see Scripture solely as the source and foundation of later interpretation. Religious and political reasons among the ancient Pharisees aided this forgetting; and the pseudepigraphical techniques of inner-biblical exegesis have served to obscure this matter yet further. It has therefore been one aim of this essay to reverse this forgetting for the sake of a historical anamnesis. The most characteristic feature of the Jewish imagination, the interpretation and rewriting of sacred texts, thus has its origin in the occasional, unsystematized instances of exegesis embedded in the Hebrew Bible, examples of which it has been my effort to recall.

·2·

EXTRA-BIBLICAL EXEGESIS: THE SENSE OF NOT READING IN RABBINIC MIDRASH

On November 24, 1644, John Milton responded to a parliamentary ordinance passed a year earlier (June 14, 1643). Control of printing was the issue, and the result was his famous *Areopagitica*. In due course, the following ironic rhetoric occurs. Since the "knowledge and survey of vice" is necessary for "the constituting of human virtue," fear of the "infection" which might arise from such study could encourage the suppression of all works which "scout into the region of sin." Among these, the Bible is particularly worrisome:

> for that [work] ofttimes relates blasphemy not nicely, it describes the carnal sense of wicked men unelegantly, it brings in honest men passionately murmuring against Providence through all the arguments of Epicurus: in other great disputes it answers dubiously and darkly to the common reader: and ask a Talmudist what ails the modesty of his marginal Keri, that Moses and all the prophets cannot persuade him to pronounce the textual Chetiv.

Here, indeed, is a point worth pondering. Among the manifest dangers of Scripture, Milton lists not only its brute descriptions of brutish men, and sundry accounts of blasphemy and desire. He also stresses the occasional paradoxes of its pronunciation—the "marginal Keri" and the "textual Chetiv." By this, Milton alludes to the rabbinic practice of substituting special (though traditional) readings for various forms found in sacred Scripture. Thus certain words are read (the *qeri*) differently from the way they are written (the *ketiv*); while in rare instances words may be read when nothing is written in Scripture at all. One therefore reads Scripture according to a fixed tradition—recorded in old Massoretic lists and the margins of printed (rabbinic) Bibles, but never in the holy scrolls themselves. In a true Derridean sense, one might say, the *qeri-ketiv* difference of the Massoretic masters is a defiant *différance:* a point where the written

19

text of the eye diverges significantly from the traditional articulation of it. Basing himself on the ancient account preserved in *Sifrei Deuteronomy* (356) and elsewhere,[1] Rabbi David Kimḥi, several centuries before Milton, had the following to say about this phenomenon in the preface to his commentary on the book of Joshua.

> It seems that these words [i.e., the *qeri* and *ketiv*] have come about because the books (of Scripture) were lost and scattered during the first exile; and the sages who were knowledgeable in Scripture had died; and the men of the Great Assembly, who restored the Torah to its previous state, found divergent readings in the books, and followed those which were supported by the majority of readings, according to their understanding [of them]. But wherever they could not decisively resolve the reading, they wrote one down but did not vocalize it, or they wrote it down in the margin but not in the text. Similarly, they sometimes inserted one reading [lit., "one way"] in the text and another in the margin.[2]

Modern scholars have not left Kimḥi's formulation as written, but have "read" its details in different ways.[3] The veracity of such historical reconstructions is not at issue here. What I rather wish to consider is the fact that, already in antiquity, scribal differences (some later formalized as *qeri-ketiv* variations) were the veritable basis for exegetical constructions of the biblical text. Two instances of this creative exchange between textual forms and midrashic formulations may suffice here.

My first example derives from a legal *derashah* (or scriptural exposition) by R. Eleazar ben R. Jose on Lev. 25:30. The biblical context deals with the sale of a dwelling in a walled town. According to the law, the original owner has the right of redemption until the end of the year of sale. After this period, however, if the property is not redeemed the regulation states that "the house in the walled town shall vest in perpetuity in the buyer and his descendents," *ve-qam ha-bayit asher lo'* (the *ketiv*) *ḥomah*. The operative portion of this rule is clearly the clause *asher lo' ḥomah*. In translating it as referring to a "house in a walled town" I have followed the traditional *qeri*, which substitutes *lo* (preposition plus pronominal suffix) for the negative particle *lo'* of the *ketiv*—thus, for the received wording "the house which is *not* in a walled town." This orthographic variation (*lo'/lo*) is fairly common in the Hebrew Bible (e.g., Exod. 21:8; Isa. 63:9), and must in many cases be due to aural errors. But given the legal or theological implications of such variants, as well as the relative contextual plausibility of one reading or another, it is striking that R. Eleazar has used *both* variants (the traditional *qeri* and *ketiv*) in his *derashah*. In *b. Megillah* 3b he states: "even though it [the town] has no [wall] now, it did have one previously." Thus the orthographic difference between *lo'* and *lo* preserved at Lev. 25:30 is not suppressed by the sage, but serves as the basis for a complex legal formulation—in which both scribal values are valorized. R. Eleazar manifestly interprets Scripture both with *and* against an official synagogal reading. The dynamic role of midrash as both a conserver and converter of tradition is thus clear.

A second example of exegetical hermeneutics rooted in textual variants comes from the aggadic, or nonlegal, sphere of midrash. As in the preceding case, the scriptural exposition in *Mishnah Soṭah* V.5 turns on a *lo'/lo* variation. R. Joshua ben Hyrkanos taught: "Job served God only out of love, as Scripture says: 'Yea, though He slay me, *lo ayaḥel*, yet will I trust in Him' (Job 13:15)." "However," he continues, "the [exegetical] meaning [of the verse] still hangs in the balance (*ve-'adayin ha-dabar shaqul*):[4] [should one understand the phrase as meaning] 'for Him, *lo*, do I wait,' or 'I do not, *lo'*, await Him?'" This query ponders whether the positive assertion of the one, or the negative grapheme of the other (the traditional *qeri* and *ketiv*) should be followed. If one opts for the first alternative, then R. Joshua's assertion about Job's piety is biblically supported. But if the negative *ketiv* is preferred, his statement seems groundless. R. Joshua resolved the matter in favor of the positive theological assertion, relying for support on the theological remark in Job 26:5, "I shall not lose my integrity until I die." In this way, a second scriptural verse from Job is used to support the primary claim of the *derashah*. On the face of it, this is an unexceptional midrashic manoeuver; and one suspects that R. Joshua has stacked his rhetorical deck for just this end. Nevertheless, the very fact that the negative formulation was raised as a serious theological possibility should not pass unnoticed. Presumably, both readings were traditional, and no one manuscript tradition was more authoritative to determine the theological issue at hand. It was only the pull of a midrashic move (the invocation here of another Joban verse) which resolved the exegetical stalemate. It would appear that R. Yoḥanan ben Zakkai never thought of this prooftext when he asserted (earlier in the text) a contrary evaluation of Job. "Job," he said, "served God only from fear (of punishment)."

In the preceding, something of the hermeneutical potential of orthographic alternatives for rabbinic exegesis was observed. The scribal variants chosen for discussion were subsequently canonized in the official *qeri-ketiv* lists of the Massoretes. But the ancient midrash also preserves homilies based on more unofficial textual variants. It is, in fact, precisely this phenomenon which explains the famous teaching of R. Ḥaninah in *b. Baba Batra* 64a—recited to this day near the close of the traditional Sabbath service. Referring to the post-exilic prophecy of Isa. 54:13, "and your sons (*banayikh*) shall enjoy great peace," he said: "Do not read 'your sons (*banayikh*),' but '*bonayikh*—your builders.'" In its full context, this new reading provides a scriptural basis for a homily asserting that "the sages increase peace (*marbim shalom*) in the world," and "there will be great peace (*shalom rab*) for the lovers of Torah." There is little doubt that these two phrases about the increase of peace reutilize the scriptural lemma "great peace (*rab shalom*)." But on what basis does R. Ḥaninah turn the whole discussion from "sons" to "builders"? Is this merely a natural association—something akin to the verbal pun found in Gen. 16:2?[5] Or might the exegetical exchange between *banayikh-bonayikh* rather be based on a scribal variant? The fact that the large Isaiah scroll found at Qumran has a hanging *vav* after the initial *beth,* so that its *banaykhi* was pronounced *bonaykhi,* argues for the second alternative. The link between Massoretic "sons" (*banayikh*) and midrashic "builders" (*bonayikh*) may therefore be assumed to be both phonetic *and* orthographic in nature.[6]

But as one will readily note, R. Ḥaninah does not just propose his new reading *bonayikh* for *banayikh.* He rather invokes it imperiously, when he says: "Do not read (*al tiqre*) 'your sons (*banayikh*),' but (*elah*) 'your builders (*bonayikh*).'" Indeed, with this exegetical formula (*al tiqre . . . elah*) we have crossed to a new hermeneutical frontier. For if in the case of genuine manuscript variants there is a traditional imperative to read what is not written (in Scripture), one may say that the *al tiqre* imperative is a midrashic instruction *not* to read what is the traditional reading of Scripture.[7] That is, midrashic teachings like R. Ḥaninah's (and they are legion) do not replace the traditional reading with a new authority; they rather suspend it playfully for the sake of the exposition—introducing difference where none was expected, and swerving a passage along a new contour of thought. And yet for all their exegetical delight, when we catch the midrashist *in flagrante delicto,* as it were, it is not so much his hermeneutical passion that excites our interest as his *passepartout:* his justification of a theological point on the basis of a biblical passage which conforms neither to the orthography nor to the sense of the original. In a word, the scriptural support is flagrantly non-scriptural in the most precise sense—for the midrashist shouts: "*al tiqre . . . elah,*" "Do not read (this) but (that)." The theological justification thus appropriates scriptural authority *mirabile dictu!*—that is to say, through the exegetical articulation of a midrashic *différance.*

I

As an exegetical phenomenon, the *al tiqre* technique is striking enough. Working at the surface of Scripture, it paradoxically reconstructs the received letters of the Bible for the sake of providing a given teaching some biblical justification. But if the explicit *al tiqre* procedure is at once both delightful and daring, the implicit use of this phenomenon excites attention in a different degree. This is so not only because the reconstruction of an *al tiqre* hermeneutic clarifies an otherwise opaque exegetical exposition. Quite frequently, this procedure is also the means for articulating some relatively radical rabbinic theology. The following bit of midrashic exegesis thematizes the point at hand. My example comes from *b. Ḥagiga* 13a, where it is reported that the elders of Pumbeditha once requested Rab Joseph bar Ḥiyya to instruct them in the esoteric "Account of the Divine Chariot." "Said he to them: 'Concerning this we were taught [in Song of Sol. 4:11]: "Honey and milk under your tongue"; [that is,] words sweeter than honey and milk should be [kept] under your tongue.' " This said, the talmudic text continues: "R. Abbahu inferred this [teaching prohibiting the public instruction of esoterica] from [Prov. 27:26]: 'lambs (*kebasim*) for your garments'; [that is,] things which are the secret of the world (*kibshono shel ʿolam*) should be [kept] under your garment."

In the printed editions of the Talmud, the hermeneutical exchange made by R. Abbahu—from "lambs for your garments" to "secret of the world"—is not explicit. It is only the manifest pun between 'lambs (*kebasim*)' and 'secrets (*kebshono*)' which suggests that the underlying biblical support for the instruction is via an implicit *al tiqre* procedure. That is to say, R. Abbahu cited the word *kebasim* (lambs) from Scripture but implied the midrashic reading *kebushim* (hidden things)—a simple enough transformation. This supposition is variously confirmed—by a manuscript tradition of this tractate,[8] by the citation of the *logion* in the *Ein Ya ʿaqov (ad loc.)*, and by the commentary of Jehuda ben Barzilai al Barceloni to the *Sepher Yetzirah*.[9] For alongside our printed Talmud text, the following reading is preserved after the citation from Proverbs: "Do not read '*kebasim*' but '*kebushim*' ": that is, "*al tiqre* lambs *elah* secret things."[10]

My purpose in bringing this example is twofold. First and foremost, it is a typical example of the implicit *al tiqre* technique. But it also provides an introduction to the fact that it is by virtue of hermeneutical strategies of substitution that more hidden scriptural meanings are disclosed. In the present context, I shall limit myself to two aspects of a mythopoetic theology imbedded in rabbinic midrash: divine empowerment through ritual praxis and divine pathos in response to human suffering.

To sharpen the context, some pertinent reflections of Gershom Scholem may be recalled at this point. Speaking of Jewish mysticism, he once observed that "[t]he whole of Aggadah," or the nonlegal aspects of rabbinic midrash, "can in a way be regarded as a popular mythology of the Jewish universe." He further added that the "mythical element which is deeply rooted in the creative forms of Aggadic production" operates on a wider, cosmic plane in the Kabbala.[11] This development is most clearly observed, he believed, in the sphere of ritual. Thus like in the Bible, where (he said) the "history-saturated ritual was accompanied by no magical action" and the "rites of remembrance produce no *effect*," "the ritual of Rabbinical Judaism [also] makes nothing happen and *transforms nothing*."[12] Both its rituals of remembrance and its rites of sanctification are "completely divorced from the solemnity of action on the mythical plane." By contrast, stressed Scholem, "nowhere does the Jewish literature of the Middle Ages bear the mythical character of these rites—except among the Kabbalists."[13]

If all this is true, it is at best a partial truth. And by this I do not simply wish to reaffirm that the aggadah is a "popular mythology of the Jewish universe." Such a characterization is, I think, an altogether weak reading of a certain portion of the midrashic corpus. While it does not entirely demote the anthropomorphic and anthropopathic imagery of midrash to mere metaphor, this perception underreads the bold production of mythopoetic exegesis in the aggadah. Indeed, such mythologizations of Scripture are often composed in support of a mythical-magical view of God and the commandments. Whether or not this theology preceded its midrashic justifications cannot gainsay the energy of its exegetical inventiveness. Something of this production and its poetics now follow.

II

The first sermon in *Pisqa* 25 of the *Pesiqta de-Rav Kahana* was composed sometime during the Days of Penitence before Yom Kippur.[14] Concerned with divine mercy and human praxis, the homily opens with Job 17:9, "But the righteous one holds fast to his way, and the pure of hands will increase [his] strength (*yosiph ometz*)." Twisting and troping the speaker initially applies the passage to God, and therewith inverts the sense of the verse. On the basis of Job's rebuttal of Eliphaz's claim (in 15:4) that his condition weakens other men's faith, the passage is now construed to yield the theological assertion that God—who is both righteous and pure of action—gives strength (*koaḥ*) to the righteous in order "that they may do His will." This construction concluded, the Joban passage is then further applied to both Moses and the righteous. On this last application, R. Azariah interprets the verse to mean: "Whenever the righteous do the will of the Holy One, Blessed be He, they increase strength (*mosiphin koaḥ*) in the *dynamis*"—that is to say, they empower the divine principle of immanent power through their performance of the commandments.[15] Quite certainly, '*something*' quite mythical (even magical) is presumed to obtain through the righteous performance of the commandments (*mitzvot*). This impression is reinforced by the scriptural prooftexts invoked to justify this assertion, as well as the corresponding disempowerment of divinity as a result of Israel's failure to do the commandments.

In support of the ritual empowerment of God through performance of the *mitzvot,* the preacher adduces Num. 14:17, "Let the strength (*koaḥ*) of the Lord be made great." This text was first invoked in the sermon to support the attribution of the opening Joban verse to Moses. In that context, the sense of the verse was interpreted to mean that Moses—a righteous one—was able to empower (*ma ʿatzim koaḥ*) God's attribute of mercy through this particular prayer. This interpretation conforms to a consistent targumic and midrashic tradition on this verse.[16] The overall notion recurs dramatically in several talmudic sources as well. For example, just this theological idea is the basis for the remarkable prayer which God is said to recite to Himself and which the divine power Akhatriel asks the High Priest Ishmael to recite *on God's behalf* when he enters the Holy of Holies on the Day of Atonement (*b. Berakhot* 7a).[17] Correspondingly, on the basis of this and related evidence, one may surmise that the reference in our homily to divine empowerment through the faithful performance of the commandments was also understood to mean the empowerment of God's attribute of mercy. Such a possibility is strengthened by the fact that this discourse was designed for the Days of Penitence before Yom Kippur.[18] In any event, this striking *theologoumenon* of ritual empowerment is complemented by the following (equally remarkable) statement: "and if not [i.e., if the commandments are not performed], [then the verse] 'You have forgotten the Rock which bore you' [Deut. 32:18, applies], as it were (*kivyakhol*)."

The prooftext is an apparent puzzle; for it is not directly obvious how this deuteronomic verse supports the assertion which precedes it. In fact, the Massoretic citation *tzur yeladekha teshi,* "you have forgotten the Rock [viz., God] which bore you," seems to have no relation to this context. What possible scriptural justification could this passage provide for the assertion that failure to perform the commandments results in a diminishment of God? Is there an exegetical connection between this "forgetting God" and the diminishment of divine power? The answer lies in the implicit *al tiqre* technique at play. For though nothing is added to the deuteronomic prooftext in this sermon, homiletical glosses found in *Leviticus Rabba* (XXIII.12) and *Sifrei Deuteronomy* (319) suggest that the verb *teshi* (you have forgotten) was midrashically construed as if it was derived from the stem *nashash* (to weaken) or *natash* (to destroy)—but *not* from the verbal stem *nashah* (to forget). Accordingly, while the assertion of divine empowerment through ritual praxis is exegetically established by reinterpreting Job 17:9 and Num. 14:17, the corresponding notion of divine depletion through ritual lassitude is scripturally justified by means of an implicit rereading of the Massoretic prooftext. One must therefore not read *teshi* (you have forgotten), but *hetashta* (you have weakened) God who bore you!

A profound theology of the commandments, with mythic-cosmic implications, is presupposed here. It hints at a dimension of ritual praxis which undoubtedly enlivened the concrete commitment to the *mitzvot* in ancient Judaism. But from the present hermeneutical perspective, what is more to the point is that the biblical justification of the foregoing rabbinic theology is in effect no biblical justification at all—so much as it is a midrashic one. In the *al tiqre* hermeneutic, the exegetical imperative is not to read Scripture as received but as revised. Midrash is thus not so much a rewritten Bible, in the manner of the book of Jubilees or pseudo-Philo's *Liber Antiquitatum Biblicarum*. It is rather a re-read Bible: readerly collusion is all. And if this is so, one may wonder (here and elsewhere) about the scriptural authority for the midrashic instructions. Indeed, one may even feel a bit like Alice, who objected to Humpty Dumpty's imperious substitution of the phrase "a nice knock-down argument" for the word "glory." If so, remember the retort: "When *I* use a word, it means just what I choose it to mean—neither more nor less." To Alice's further query about whether one "*can* make words mean different things," the resourceful Humpty Dumpty countered: "The question is which is to be master—that's all."

The hermeneutical issue may be sharpened. Granting that no rabbinic midrashist would ever intend his interpretative act to dispossess the scriptural authority of the Bible, one must ponder all the more just how the sages asserted their exegetical authority over the text—to echo Mr. Dumpty's retort. The answer for the case at hand (Deut. 32:18) lies, I think, in the word *kivyakhol*—translated earlier by "as it were." On the face of it, this term appears to be a pious gloss on the mythical midrash at hand—a kind of rational disclaimer, signifying that the acute anthropopathic assertions about God should not be taken literally. Recalling the exposition in Deut. 32:18, one might therefore claim that the pointed use of *kivyakhol* serves to weaken the bold notion that ritual failure diminishes God—to say that this theology is only adduced *als ob*, 'as if' one could suppose such a thing. In fact, and for understandable reasons, this has been the explanation of the word *kivyakhol* in the long history of its exegesis—from Rashi's talmudic glosses (e.g., *b. Yoma* 3b) to the researches of N. Bruell[19] and W. Bacher.[20] But if *kivyakhol* is in fact a rational disclaimer for exegetical daring, we must still wonder why such mythopoetic midrash was invoked in the first place. Why assert (about God) with one breath what one feels constrained to withdraw with another? Why open your mouth to temptation at all?

The solution to the exegetical issue is less convoluted. The use of *kivyakhol* in classical midrash is in fact no poor man's piety but the heroics of rabbinic hermeneutics. It provides a way of becoming master of the text and its theology while simultaneously acknowledging the independent authority of Scripture. Indeed a full review of the evidence suggests that whenever the word *kivyakhol* is used—and it is used primarily in assertions about God—it functions to indicate that *if* one reads the biblical passage midrashically, such and so is the sense which *can be* construed.[21] That is to say: the formula *kivyakhol* means, quite literally, "as it were" or "if one may suppose"; but it serves to introduce a reading of Scripture built by a midrashic construction, usually of the (implicit) *al tiqre* type. Thus by way of example, let us return to the midrashic exposition of Deut. 32:18 cited earlier. It may be freely paraphrased as follows: "If you do not perform the commandments, then concerning you the scriptural phrase *tzur yeladekha teshi* applies; for it can be understood to mean, *as it were:* 'you have weakened God (the Rock) who bore you.'" In this and many other examples, it is not wrong to say that Scripture justifies the midrashic instruction at hand. One must only stress that it does so *kivyakhol:* only on the strength of the exegete's bold rereading of it.

<hr>

III

Among the modalities of mythopoetic midrash, two have been isolated for consideration: those expressing theologies of divine empowerment, and those dealing with divine pathos. As with the preceding example, the following expositions also utilize the term *kivyakhol* in conjunction with the (implicit) *al tiqre* method. I shall start with an example of historical pathos.

Exodus Rabba (XXX.24) preserves a dense but expressive exegesis of the phrase *ki qeroba yeshu'ati lavo'*, "for My salvation is near to come" (Isa. 56:1). In its primary context, God simply announces the imminent advent of His salvation. Accordingly, the pronoun suffix of *yeshu'ati* (/ti/) functions as a straightforward objective genitive; that is to say, "My salvation" means the act of salvation which God (the speaker) will bring about. However, in the course of the exposition, this sense is inverted. With deceptively naive literalism, the midrashist construes the suffix as a subjective genitive, so that the text now projects an image of God's own salvation. He begins with a philologist's observation: "Scripture does not say '*your* salvation' (second person plural) but '*My* salvation.'" And he adds: "May His Name be blessed! For were it not [so] written [in Scripture], one could not say it (*ilulei sheha-dabar katub iy ephshar le-'omero*)." What is the point? Why does the midrashist belabor the grammatical *différance* between 'My' and 'your' salvation if the sense is semantically straightforward? The answer unfolds in the continuation of the *derashah*, where God is made to say: "If you [Israel] do not have merit, I shall perform [the salvation] for My *own* sake (*bishvili*); for *kivyakhol*, as long as you are in trouble I am with you, as it says [in Scripture]: 'I am with him (Israel) in trouble ('*imo anokhi be-tzarah*)' (Ps. 91:15). And [further]: I will redeem Myself, as it says:... 'Rejoice greatly, O daughter of Jerusalem...; [for] behold your king comes unto you: He is righteous and *nosha*', victorious (Zech. 9:9).'" After citing this last prooftext, the midrashist adds another textual observation. "Scripture does not write *moshi*'a (a savior) but *nosha*' (is saved)," he says; and with this philological flourish the rhetor rounds off his exegetical proof that the Isaianic verse (*ki keroba yeshu*'*ati lavo*') means "*My* salvation is near to come."

If "salvation is near to come," the hermeneutical process of this midrash is far from forthcoming. The clue lies in the conjunction of the formula *ilulei sheha-dabar katub* ("were it not [so] stated in Scripture") with the term *kivyakhol*. When this occurs, the midrashic sense of the lemma is derived by reinflecting the written grapheme (the *dabar katub:* 'Scripture' in the literal sense) in anthropomorphic or anthropopathic ways. The received letters or vowels of Scripture remain intact. As a result, new sense is not construed through a semiotic refiguration of the forms of Scripture, but by their semantic reemphasis. As the midrashist in this *derashah* has stressed the significance of the pronominal suffix /*ti*/, and has also emphasized God's involvement in Israel's suffering and salvation, it is clear that his reinterpretation of the Isaianic verse hinges upon reading *yeshu*'*ati* as a noun plus a *subjective* genitive. Thus one is expected to read "*My own* salvation is near to come," not "*My* salvation is near to come." The midrash on Isa. 56:1 thus unfolds by means of an implicit *al tiqre* procedure which semantically rereads "what is written in Scripture" in a daring theological way.

The same hermeneutical logic underlies the other prooftexts in this homiletical unit. For example, whereas the passage from Ps. 91:15 ('*imo anokhi be-tzarah*) would ordinarily be construed to mean "I (God) shall be with him (Israel) in his suffering," now, under the pressure of the midrashic rereading of *yeshu*'*ati*, these words are correspondingly reinflected to mean: "I [God] will be with Israel sufferingly (*betzarah*)"; that is, in shared pathos. A similar exegetical pressure affects the final proof of the exposition, which cites Zech. 9:9 and adds the observation that "Scripture does not write *moshi*'a but *nosha*'." Now since one would have naturally expected an active participle like *moshi*'a (savior) to correspond to the first noun *tzaddik* (righteous), the specific use of the passive-reflexive participle *nosha*' (is saved) can only confirm for the midrashist that God's own salvation is textually marked in Scripture. Thus, once again the hermeneutical term *kivyakhol* signals a daring reinflection of the traditional sense and sensibility of Scripture. And once again the Bible is troped against itself to produce a myth of divine pathos.

In other midrashic texts, this co-suffering of God and Israel is personalized through a *mythos* of divine compassion for human pain. A striking example occurs in *Mishnah Sanhedrin* (VI.4). In this text, an historical episode about capital punishment by hanging is reported. Added to it is the practice of removing a hanged corpse before nightfall, in fulfillment of the negative commandment (Deut. 21:23): "His body shall not remain all night upon the tree; but thou shalt surely bury him the same day, for he that is hanged is a curse against God (*ki qilelat elohim talui*)." The precise meaning of this rule was a matter of ancient legal discussion, as is attested by the exegetical discussions of it preserved in the so-called *Temple Scroll*. In part, the issue turned on whether the regulation prescribes death by hanging or hanging (for show and shame) after the death penalty was administered by some other means.[22] In any case, it is the motivation clause appended to the biblical rule which elicits successive midrashic expositions at the conclusion of our mishnah. The first of these, following the aforementioned case of capital punishment (for witchcraft), interprets the biblical phrase "for he that is hanged is a curse against God" to mean: he that is hanged [is so punished because] he cursed [the Name of] God. This comment is itself the result of a bold hermeneutical manoeuver. But our attention for present purposes is rather drawn to the very next mishnah (VI.5) where another—more remarkable—interpretation is provided. We read: "Rabbi Meier said: 'When a person is in grave trouble (*mitzṭaʿer*), what does the *Shekhinah* say? [It says] *kivyakhol:* "My head is in pain, my arm is in pain (*qallani me-roshi, qallani mi-yadi*).'"

What is involved here? What is the relation between the human suffering in the first part of Rabbi Meier's remark and the divine sympathy subsequently asserted about the *Shekhinah*—God's indwelling presence? Once more the clue lies with the word *kivyakhol*. As elsewhere, this term introduces a blatant anthropopathism into the midrash and signals an implicit *al tiqre* hermeneutic. The result is that our scriptural verse ("for he that is hanged is a curse against God, *ki qilelat elohim talui*") is radically reappropriated to support a theology of divine pathos. Between the lemma and the teaching is a midrashic reading which runs something like this: "for a hanged one [viz., a human in distress] is a *qilelat* of God; [however,] do not read *qilelat elohim*, a curse of God, but *qallat elohim*, the pain of God."

It is a secondary matter here that the key verb *qalal* must be euphemistically construed in order for the midrash to make sense. The central hermeneutical fact is rather that Deut. 21:23 serves to express a midrashic *mythologoumenon* of divine suffering. Remarkably, by the merest exegetical allowance, we find that Scripture enfolds a *mythos* of divine care in an old casuistic construction. So delicate, indeed, is the thread of discourse that the merest rattle of the midrashic shuttle weaves a texture of compassion around a stern legal rule. In this way, a motivation clause which advocates the removal of a hanged corpse because of the horrific blasphemy involved reveals the shudder of divine anguish at human suffering. The readerly collusion between midrashist and audience thus stands exposed for all its hermeneutical power. More precisely: through his punning allusion to a shared lemma (*qallani* alludes to *qilelat elohim*), the exegete involves the reader in the active process of midrashic production. Accepting the intertextual invitation, the addressee may reenact the exegete's own rereading of the biblical text—in the manner of a midrashic mimesis, which moves from a shared Scripture to its shared reauthoring. In this process also lies the reauthorization of Torah for the community as a whole.

Let me now trope the preceding instances of mythical midrash with a final example. It extends the readerly collusion between exegete and reader one twist more. The text is found in *Sifrei Bemidbar (Beha'alotekha), Pisqa* 84.[23] Starting with the biblical phrase *ve-yanusu mis'aneykha*, "And may Your enemies (O Lord) be routed" (Num. 10:35), the comments successively turn on the pivot of God's enemies. The midrash opens with the comment that "anyone who hates Israel—as it were (*ke'ilu*) hates the Creator"; the point is concluded with appropriate prooftexts. The midrash then adds: "and anyone who rises against Israel—as it were (*ke'ilu*) rises against God." After several prooftexts, the following verse from Zechariah (2:12) is adduced: "for whoever hurts you [viz., Israel] is like one who hurts his own eye (*ke-noge'a be-babat 'eyno*)." On this verse, Rabbi Judah said: "Scripture does not say '[who hurts] an eye (*be-babat 'ayin*),' but 'his [very own] eye (*be-babat 'eyno*).'" And he adds: "Scripture is directed, *kivyakhol*, toward God, but it has been euphemistically modified (*elah she-kinah ha-katub*)." There then follows a whole list of cases where Scripture has been putatively changed because, otherwise, the formulation about God would appear unseemly. These are the famous cases of scribal corrections, also known as *tiqqunei sopherim*.[24]

Just what about Zech. 2:12 was theologically disrespectful? The exegetical mote is apparently the anthropomorphic simile that is used: "for whosoever hurts you *is like* one who hurts his own eye (*'eyno*)." But there is really nothing in this phrase which even remotely requires euphemistic correction. The simile seems quite neutral: "his eye" refers to the eye of the avenger, who, by hurting Israel, hurts himself as well. It is only the mythopoetic theology of the midrash which produces a hypothetical reconstruction of an assumed uncorrected text—one in which God presumably said: "Whoever hurts Israel is like one who hurts *My* eye (i.e.,

ʿeyni for *ʿeyno*)." The midrashist in fact acknowledges this rabbinic reconstruction, for he invokes the word *kivyakhol*—his index of a hypothetical
reading—before citing the prooftext from Zechariah.

Now since none of the other biblical texts adduced as euphemistic
revisions deal with this theme of divine pathos, and also since none of
them use the word *kivyakhol*, I am inclined to suppose that they are all
intrusive in this midrash. This supposition is further supported by the
existence (in different forms in the different manuscripts) of a repetition
of R. Judah's midrash (along with the word *kivyakhol*) after the list of texts,
in the manner of an editorial resumption which brackets a literary inter-
polation.[25] One may therefore contend that at least our Zecharian passage (among other prooftexts) is a midrash, and no scribal correction in
the exact sense.[26] For R. Judah's comment presupposes that we do not
read "his eye (*ʿeyno*)" with the received Massoretic text, but "My eye (*ʿeyni*)"
as the midrashic subtext. In comparison with other examples of the *al tiqre*
phenomenon, the brazenness of the midrashic manoeuver here is that the
hermeneutical construction does not hypothecate a *new* text but dares to
assert an *original* Scripture. It would seem that midrashic authority and
textual authorship get confused in this instance. But let us not be doubly
duped. We were duly warned: *kivyakhol*.

IV

In the course of these reflections, I have referred to a readerly collusion
between the exegetical speaker and the addressee. *Do not read* this *but* that,
we hear; *al tiqre* this word *elah* that one. Repeatedly, a will to theological
power through textuality has reformed and reimagined Scripture. Indeed the markings of *kivyakhol* are nothing if they are not also the signs of
hermeneutical desire: the imaginative shaping of the letters of Scripture
in accordance with theological will. Midrashic projection thus seems to
qualify as a majestic mimesis, an exegetical tracing of thought along the
curve of God's letters for the sake of divinizing human desire. Slowly, one
reading after another, the words of Scripture are re-formed and re-united
into a new corpus: Midrash.

To what may this be compared? To the scattered fragments of Osiris,
which were gathered up by Isis in her patient wanderings over the land.
This old myth, probably in the form retold by Plutarch, was itself compared by Milton (also in the *Areopagitica*) to the destruction of virgin
Truth—whose "lovely form" was hewed "into a thousand pieces, and
scattered to the four winds. From that time ever since, the sad friends of
Truth, such as durst appear, imitating the careful search that Isis made
for the mangled body of Osiris, went up and down gathering limb by

limb, still as they could find them." Strange to say, this account of Isis and Osiris is almost certainly the basis of the wonderful midrash in the *Mekhilta de-Rabbi Ishmael (Vayehi Beshallaḥ,* 1) dealing with Moses' recovery of the bones of Joseph—buried in the Nile.[27] According to this legend, the casket containing Joseph's bones arose from the hidden depths after Moses inscribed a gold tablet with God's Holy Name (the *Shem Ha-Mephorash*) and threw it into the river while reciting an adjuration.[28] However, Do not read *Shem Ha-Mephorash,* the Explicitly Articulated Name of God, but the *shem ha-mepharesh!*—the nouns and words which are interpreted by the descendents of Moses. These are the words of Midrash, which are joined to Scripture as bone is joined to bone—so that a new creation be formed, *kivyakhol.*

·3·

THE GARMENTS OF TORAH—OR, TO WHAT MAY SCRIPTURE BE COMPARED?

In recent years, there has been a growing concern in various literary circles to accord Scripture the status of a privileged text—that is, the status of specialness which was once called sanctity. Now, such a hermeneutical move should at least raise some eyebrows in this day and age when, after centuries of benign or not so benign neglect, and after the rise of new literary attitudes and canons, Scripture has been apparently put 'in its place'—as but one corpus of national texts among all their ancient Near Eastern and Hellenistic congeners. No one factor has reversed this process of neutralization; just as no one factor has catalyzed the recent renaissance of secular interest in the Bible. Still, it may not be entirely misguided to suspect that the new concern to privilege Scripture within the acknowledged literary canon of our culture may be motivated in part by a desire to provide a challenge to modern literature, where such notions of 'specialness' and 'sanctity' are conspicuously and determinately absent. Indeed, for many moderns all texts are complexly textured by the threads of all predecessor texts and by the play of differences inherent in language itself. There is never a first thread in this garment that may be pulled loose; for there is no paradigm text, no Logos. Accordingly, the reemergence of Scripture to the privileged status of a pivotal and generative literary code presumably serves to recenter our Western cultural enterprise and its creativity. Some critics have even begun to query whether there may in fact be something specific to the biblical text which gives it this re-found specialness.

Amid all this breathless activity it would therefore seem salutary to pause for some historical air, and ask: Where would such features as might constitute the specialness of Scripture lie, and how would one ever begin to find them—particularly if one started with literary categories and criteria drawn from secular literary criticism, and not from our traditional religious cultures where the tasks of reading and textual analysis have been altogether different? For me and I suspect for many other moderns, no matter how well disposed, the possibility of proving the ontological uniqueness or privilege of Scripture from its very nature— and not from secondary attributions—seems either hopeless or tendentious, or both. But there were other times in our cultural past when such a polemical challenge would have been taken up with confident glee—and these may serve to refocus the discussion from an enlarged perspective. A most striking instance of just such a polemic is preserved in a Jewish mystical text from thirteenth-century Spain. The passage responds to Averroistic trends in certain Jewish circles which regarded many biblical narratives as crude stories, and many biblical laws as symbolic truths only. The result is a powerful attempt to privilege Scripture on the basis of a "myth of Torah."

> Rabbi Simeon said: If a man looks upon the Torah as merely a book presenting narratives and everyday matters, alas for him! Such a torah, one treating with everyday concerns, and indeed a more excellent one, we too, even we, could compile. More than that, in the possession of the rulers of the world there are books of even greater merit, and these we could emulate if we wished to compile some such torah. But the Torah, in all of its worlds, holds supernal truths and sublime secrets. . . .
>
> [Indeed,] the Torah it was that created the angels and created all the worlds and through Torah are all sustained. The world could not endure the Torah if she had not garbed herself in garments of this world.
>
> Thus the tales related in the Torah are simply her outer garments, and woe to the man who regards that outer garb as the Torah itself, for such a man will be deprived of portion in the next world. Thus David said: "Open Thou mine eyes, that I may behold wondrous things out of Thy law" (Ps. 119:18), that is to say, the things that are underneath. See now. The most visible part of a man are the clothes that he has on, and they who lack understanding, when they look at the man, are apt not to see more in him than these clothes. In reality, however, it is the body of the man that constitutes the pride of his clothes, and his soul constitutes the pride of his body.
>
> So it is with the Torah. Its narrations which relate to things of the world constitute the garments which clothe the body of the Torah; and that body is composed of the Torah's precepts, *gufey-torah* (bodies, major principles). People without understanding see only the narrations, the garment; those somewhat more penetrating see also the body. But the truly wise, those who serve the most high King and stood on mount Sinai, pierce all the way through to the soul, to the true Torah which is the root principle of all. These same will in the future be vouchsafed to penetrate to the very soul of the soul of the Torah. . . .
>
> Woe to the sinners who look upon the Torah as simply tales pertaining to things of the world, seeing thus only the outer garment. But the righteous whose gaze penetrates to the very Torah, happy are they. Just as wine must be in a jar to keep, so the Torah must be contained in an

outer garment. That garment is made up of the tales and stories; but we, we are bound to penetrate beyond. (*Zohar*, III.152)[1]

As is trenchantly stated here, Hebrew Scripture is an ontologically unique literature: not because of its aesthetic style or topics of concern—which are judged weak in comparison with contemporary medieval romances and epics—but precisely because such externalities are merely the first of several garment-like layers concealing deeper and less-refracted aspects of divine truth whose core, the root of all roots, is God himself. Thus, as is indicated in this myth of scriptural origin, the divine Reality exteriorizes and condenses itself, at many removes from its animating soul-root, into a verbal text with several layers of meaning. The true hermeneut—who is a seeker after God and not simply a purveyor of aesthetic tropes or normative rules—will be drawn to this garmented bride (as the Torah is called in another text in this corpus) and will strip away the garments of Torah until he and the beloved one (God as discovered in the depths of Scripture) are one. Seen thus, the goal of interpretation is an ecstatic *hieros gamos* of sorts, and the successive hermeneutical penetrations to deeper and less veiled truths may be compared to a spiritual rite of passage. "Such a man," says another Zoharic text (II.99a–b), "is . . . a 'bridegroom of the Torah' in the strictest sense . . . to whom she (divinity as beckoning Bride) discloses all her secrets, concealing nothing."

Let me put the matter slightly differently. The Bible is proclaimed sacred by our mystical author not just because it communicates divine teachings in a narrative or legal form, but precisely because these teachings are not constituted by language in any ordinary sense. Indeed, these narratives and laws are but a species of the divine Logos which radiates from the inmost center of divinity: a tangible exteriorization of divinity providing the symbolic map for the human spiritual journey that may culminate in communion with the most inward truth of God. On this view the Bible, compared to a veiled body or bride, is ontologically unique principally because it is nothing less than a dimension of divinity itself. The words of a later kabbalist, R. Abraham Azulai, may sum up these various reflections while providing a hint of the deep simultaneity that may exist between textual study and spiritual quest.

> . . . the Torah [in this world] is robed in a material garment just like mankind [in its corporeal condition]. But when mankind will rise up from its physical condition to a more subtle [spiritual] state, so will the material manifestation of the Torah be altered and its spiritual essence be apprehended in ever higher levels of reality . . . [Then] the con-

cealed faces of the Torah will shine and the righteous will meditate on them. But in all this the Torah remains one [and the same] . . . [for] its essence never changes. (*Ḥesed le-Abraham*, II,11)

Let me, for the moment, suspend my discussion of Jewish mystical meditations on Scripture and recall some of the notions of a sacred text that originate in biblical antiquity and among the sages of ancient Judaism. Such a detour will, I think, put matters in a fuller historical and hermeneutical perspective.

I

In ancient Israel—before, indeed, the Bible was the Bible—its laws, teachings, prophecies, and so on were given prestige by the authority of the divine voice that reportedly spoke them directly or indirectly (through assorted mouthpieces and filters); or, as in the case of the epic and historical narratives, this prestige principally accrued from the very invisibility and obliquity of the speaker (in a manner well-known to students of Benveniste).[2] But the prestige of these narrative traditions also accrued quite early—as we know from Ps. 78:5 and the prologue to Deuteronomy—by virtue of their textual association with the legal and ethical teachings given via the divine voice, as revelations. Now this complex process, whereby materials of quite ordinary levels of authority and content were gradually raised to the highest prestige through their literary contextualization with divine revelations more centrally located or regarded in the cultural corpus, is one of the paradoxical by-products of what we now call the formation of the canon. The early rabbis were certainly aware of these matters in their discussions of different levels of authority in Scripture; and one may note in passing that the processes reflected in the Jewish Hellenistic text called *Wisdom of Sirach*—where many of the secular proverbs of the Hebrew Bible were infused with nomistic allusions—only show how early the attempt to assimilate all valued teachings to the core revelations of Sinai can be documented, but say nothing about the long processes which preceded them in Israelite antiquity.

As the rabbis gradually circumscribed and closed the corpus of biblical traditions in the first centuries of our era, two notable aspects bearing on the sense—and gradually on the juridical fact—of the Bible's sanctity deserve special mention. The first bears on the strict rules laid down for how the Pentateuch—that portion of Scripture with the highest authority for Judaism—must be written and with what material means. Clearly, the Five Books of Moses were not to be books like other books in either shape or form; and the rules pertaining to their treatment, preservation, and even rescue in times of danger (as e.g., if a fire occurred on the Sabbath day) were quite different from rules relating to all other books—especially the works of *Homeros,* Homer, which the rabbis demoted to a "secular document" and punningly compared to a *ḥamor,* or donkey (cf. *Mishnah Yadaim* IV.6).[3] Indeed, in these legal contexts the ancient Pharisees attributed a special *cultic* sanctity to Holy Scripture, especially the Pentateuch. Such sacred texts could in fact "defile the hands," and so were dealt with as part of the priestly system of holiness and contagion.[4] No matter that this attribution may in fact derive from venal contestations for power. The fact remains that we begin to see in these initial centuries the dignification of the written word of God with an aura nearly commensurate in mystery and power with the living divine voice which it replaces. In a word, so to speak, the increased exoteric sanctity of the text *as text* at this time, and the transfer to it of the regimen of priestly holiness and safeguards, correspond quite remarkably with the displacement of the living divine presence by a textual record of that presence. The powerful and empowering aura of a sanctified Torah text thus concealed a profound absence at its deepest core.

This leads to a related point. Of considerable importance in the sanctification of Scripture is that the prestigious literary canon of divine teachings had become a *closed literary corpus*—one culturally reopened only through human textual exegesis. The early Pharisees fully comprehended this paradoxical and dialectical fact, and began to search the Scriptures in every possible way for every possible prolongation of the original divine teachings in new times. Thus, the entirety of Scripture was spread out before the sages as the exoteric content which could be verbally recombined, analogically juxtaposed, or even harmoniously synthesized in myriad ways to make the old written Torah a "living Torah" again. Now, since all depended on exegesis, it was fateful in this period— just as in later ones—*just which* hermeneutical agenda was accepted and *just how* and to *what extent* the core texts were compared. As is well known, the Pharisees developed a distinctive form of oral exegesis which gave renewed authority to the written Torah. But precisely because this system of exegesis was geared to establishing the normative religious praxes of the Jews, which included many rules of sacred activity, it was only to be expected that the textual source of the sacred praxes of the Jews was *itself* reenfranchised with an even deeper juridical sanctity and authority. Thus the textual sanctity of Scripture is signalled by its status not only as the preserved verbal traces of an older divine communication, but—for the Pharisees, at least—as the source of ever-new revelations and guidance *through living interpretations of it.* In the words of a midrashic comment: "When the Holy One, blessed be He, gave the Torah to Israel, He only gave it as wheat from which to extract flour, and as flax wherewith to weave a garment through [the hermeneutical principles of deduction called] *klal u-phrat, prat u-khlal,* and *klal u-phrat u-khlal"* (*Eliyahu Zutta,* II). Interpretation, therefore, partakes of the sanctity of Scripture even as it further reveals it: for the role of interpretation is neither aesthetic illumination nor aesthetic judgment, but rather the religious duty to expound and extend, and so to *reactualize* the ancient word of God for the present hour.

These matters deserve a more ramified discussion than the present context permits; so let me add to the preceding discussion only those few points that may develop our inquiry into the remarkable notions of sanctity that gradually accrued to Scripture. The first point to be stressed is that, with their exegetical procedures—the rabbis would say, *precisely because of their exegetical procedures*—the early Pharisees revealed unexpected possibilities in the original divine communication. It was gradually claimed that "all is in it" (*Mishnah 'Abot* V.25)—or better, that all could be recovered from it if one but had the appropriate hermeneutical key. The upshot of this is that the rabbis were, quite early, conscious and articulate about the fact that the divine communication in the Torah was not a communication like any human one. It was, rather, a unique or special communication: a *Sondersprache.* Now, to be sure, for these rabbis of late antiquity the singularity of Scripture did not lie in the notion that the text was *part* and *parc*el of the divine nature (like the mystical text cited earlier) but lay rather in the depth of possibilities for true teaching, the legal and theological experience, latent in the text. This exegetical latency, in fact, was felt to be part of the ontological nature of Scripture—and so the very warp and woof of its sanctity.

Let me develop this point of latent meanings in Scripture a bit further: for it is the issue of *levels* of truth that, already in antiquity, gives our subject a new edge and vitality. As we have seen, the early rabbinic sages were preoccupied with exploring the plurivocity of the biblical text and the sacred behaviors and theologoumena generated out of it through the agency of their sacred interpretative procedures—that is, procedures they believed to be divinely sanctioned. From texts like the *Damascus Document* from Qumran in the first century B.C.E. through *Canticles Rabba* centuries later, the Torah was likened to an inexhaustible well of vivifying waters.[5] And in many midrashic comments of these years, the act of interpretation was itself given theophanic proportions, insofar as the later-day interpreter was said to stand at Sinai *in the course of his exegesis.* There is thus a profound modality of myth and ritual that should not go unnoticed here—or in any discussion of Judaism, for that matter—insofar as the praxis of interpretation participates in the timeless-yet-timeful realm of the foundational *mythos* (Torah), and insofar as the exegetical praxis reactualizes the *mythos* in the communal here and now. And here, too, something else must not go unnoticed: namely, that the reactualization of the *mythos* (Torah) via interpretation is not simply a repetition of it but a profound transformation of its meanings. Accordingly, in the ritual scenario of sacred interpretation there is something akin to the well-known dynamic of "violence and the sacred": for an exegetical violence is done to the plain-sense of the sacred text for the very sake of saving and serving its acknowledged sanctity. In this feast of particles and pronouns the act of violence is naturally repressed for the most part and represented as the sanctioned means of allowing the innate fulness of the divine text to be mediated historically. In a sense, the exegetical violence is domesticated, even sacralized, we may say, by means of the restraining forms of religiously legitimate interpretation.

Philo of Alexandria, who flourished at roughly the same time as such early rabbinic sages as Hillel of Palestine, adds another coal to the fire. For while his contemporary ben Bag Bag already proclaimed that "all" was in Scripture—meaning that everything necessary for a complete religious life was in the Torah—Philo spoke of the *hyponoia* of Scripture: its deep inner sense which could be disclosed via allegorical techniques. Thus for Philo and other philosophical allegorists, like Maimonides over a millenium later, who spoke of the *baṭin*, or inward truth of the text, the fulness of Scripture went beyond its external 'plain-sense' and included the truths of Stoic or Aristotelian or neo-Platonic thought. The remarkable truth of Scripture was thus that it contained an exterior divine communication which could sponsor, at one and the same time, both the normative sacred behaviors of Judaism and the universal truths of philosophical reason. Surely ben Bag Bag in provincial Palestine would have been most amazed to learn that *so much* was "in it." But for Philo and Maimonides such a disclosure only enhanced the inherent sacrality of Scripture. Moreover, since "all was in it," nothing was outside it either—so that a Jew could remain a Jew (reading Scripture according to its plain-sense and for its traditional legal-theological teachings) and be a philosopher to boot. Nothing had to be sacrificed: revelation and reason were joined in the unique plurivocity of Scripture. Looking at this hermeneutics a bit differently, we might even summarize the achievement of Philo and Maimonides by saying that it Judaized Stoic and Aristotelian wisdom, so that old Aristotle was *really* divine—as Maimonides and others suggested—and had within him an anticipatory touch of the sacred revelation granted Moses. Surely you will have caught here more than a faint Jewish echo of the well-known *interpretatio Christiana*, by means of which Virgil and other pagans were accommodated by the Church Fathers into the normative Christian fold insofar as their writings were shown to "anticipate" the real good news—albeit through a glass darkly.[6]

All of this suggests that for medieval Jews and Christians the inherent sanctity of Scripture could radiate outward and include books thoroughly *extra ecclesia* and give them *salus*. Nor should this seem altogether surprising; for men like Augustine or Gregory or Maimonides show not a little straying after false gods—be they the superior poetry of Virgil or the superior philosophy of Aristotle—and it was good to know in the end that this was really a "sacred" lust, insofar as the gods of secular scriptures were shown to have been graced by the God of Abraham. And not only this, but a distinct sanctity could also radiate out from sacred Scripture to books acknowledged faithfully to interpret it. In the Jewish orbit one thinks first of the Mishnah and Talmud as the primary examples, and one may even add here the works of the principal medieval commentators, like Rashi, whose comments were transmitted and later printed alongside the holy Torah itself. In sixteenth-century Palestine, in fact, the holy power of the law code of the Mishnah was such that some mystics actually recited it as a mantra in order to induce the appearance of a celestial mentor;[7] and the sacred status of the Zohar for Sephardi Jews in particular, and the role it played in recitations by Yemenite Jews (who in all cases did not even understand its arcane contents) is a matter of historical record.[8]

A more paradoxical but nonetheless deeply instructive example of the principle we have been pursuing here may be found in the late Jewish Renaissance work called *Nophet Ṣuphim* by Judah ben Yeḥiel Messer Leon. I use the word "paradoxical" in this regard not because Messer Leon exemplifies the rhetoric of Aristotle, Quintilian, and Cicero with, as he says, "illustrations . . . adduce[d] from our own glorious sanctuary"—that is, the Bible—but because he contended that the secular "science of Rhetoric" (*ḥokhmat ha-ḥalatzah*) was decisive for a proper understanding of sacred writ. Let us hear the point in his own words:

> Every science and every rationally apprehended truth that any treatise may contain is present in our Holy Torah and in the Books of those who speak by the Holy Spirit. . . . In the days of Prophecy, indeed, *in the months of old* (Job 29:2), when *out of Zion, the perfection of beauty, God shined forth* (Ps. 50:2), we used to learn and know from the Holy Torah all the sciences and truths of reason, including all that were humanly attained, for everything is either latent therein, or plainly stated. . . . But after the indwelling Presence of God departed from our midst because of our many iniquities . . . we were no longer able to derive understanding of all scientific developments from the Torah's words; this condition, however, persists due to our own falling short, our failure to know the Torah in full perfection. Thus the matter has come to be in reverse; for if, after we have come to know all the sciences, or some part of them, we study

the words of the Torah, then the eyes of our understanding open to the fact that the sciences are included in the Torah's words, and we wonder how we could have failed to realize this from the Torah itself to begin with. Such has frequently been our experience, especially in the science of Rhetoric. For when I examined the words of the Torah in the way now common amongst most people, I had no idea that the science of Rhetoric or any part of it was included therein. But once I had studied and investigated Rhetoric, *searched for her as for hidden treasures* (Prov. 2:4) out of the treatises written by men of nations other than our own, and afterwards came back to see what is said of her in the Torah and the Holy Scriptures, then *the eyes* of my understanding *were opened* (Gen. 3:7), and I saw that it is the Torah which was the giver. . . . and I marvel how previously *the Spirit of the Lord passed* (1 Kings 22:24) me by, so that I did *not know her place, where it is* (Nah. 3:17). (Bk. I. ch. 13. 12–13)[9]

In this striking formulation, Messer Leon argues that Holy Scripture comprehends *all* wisdom, and that for him, recourse to the Gentile rhetoricians was both a necessary and propaedeutic detour—because the ancient Jewish *ars rhetorica* had been deemed lost among the Jews. (In a somewhat comparable way, the great Maimonides also believed that this allegorical method was a revival of a lost antique tradition.) But if Cicero's *Rhetorica ad Herrenium* is a valid means of interpreting Scripture, has not Messer Leon gone a long way toward bridging the gap between secular and sacred writ? Or should we rather say that secular Cicero is valid only when his rhetorical structures can be shown to lie immanently within Holy Scripture itself? I should myself perhaps incline toward the latter alternative, for it tallies with the more widespread teaching in Jewish literary history that I have been reviewing; namely, that the Bible is an ontologically unique document insofar as it is deemed the *only* comprehensive text we have—stratified as it is into multiple layers of truth, and so truly a "word" worthy of a god. There is thus no need for the creative artist or thinker to produce new imaginative realities. God's Torah comprehends them all. The dictum "all is in it" has, as I suggested earlier, its corollary in the realization that "nothing is outside it." The death of Virgil is thus his resurrection in Scripture.

II

We are now ready to return, somewhat belatedly, to our opening mystical meditation. For if the exoteric rabbinical tradition was concerned properly to understand the divine will in its ongoing historical revelation to Israel, and thus to see the sanctity of Scripture in its divine origin and norm-establishing powers; and if the allegorical tradition was concerned to understand the divine wisdom in its eternal and nonhistorical truth for all reasonable persons, and thus to regard the uniqueness of Scripture as its capacity to teach simultaneously at various cognitive levels; the esoteric tradition of Judaism was concerned to encounter the presence of God, and thus to see the special sanctity and uniqueness of Scripture in its being at once a hieroglyph of the divine Logos *and* divine Reality itself. God is not merely present in Scripture through a kind of verbal displacement. God and Scripture are, in fact, one mysterious and inseparable Truth. Scripture is thus nothing less than the immediacy of God in a verbal "expression."

Over and over again in classical Spanish Kabbala and its aftermath we find the image that the Torah is cloaked in several garments of concealment, an image used to express the vision of the primordial processes of divinity originating in supernal realms as only progressively exteriorized into less spiritual forms until finally coming to symbolic expression in the Torah which we now have on this earth. In its origin, then, the Torah is a true *Sondersprache*—a text containing within itself, from the beginning, the absolute plenitude of divine Being. Correspondingly, the Torah remains a *Sondersprache* in its historical, Sinaitic form, as well, since it is really *multum in parvo:* the infinity of divine Being in a condensed linguistic expression. This, then, is the ontological uniqueness of the Torah from the esoteric point of view. And so, following the Plotinean scheme, the first task of a reader is to be spiritually converted to the divine plenitude symbolically distilled in Scripture, and then, by means of a mystical hermeneutics, to disrobe the bride in order to unite with her behind her many veils. From the speech of God one is thus led to divinity itself: for in Scripture the divine Logos *is* divinity in its various concealments. This being so, many Jewish mystics were not even afraid to speak of these garments as the names of God, so that for them the Torah is nothing but a series of permutations on the divine Name—which is the same as divine Reality. In a striking variant of the Zoharic passage noted earlier, which culminates in an ecstatic encounter with divinity as the bedecked Bride of Torah, R. Joseph Chiquatilla portrays a corresponding process whereby divinity as the enrobed King of Torah progressively casts off his garments as the mystic penetrates beyond the external forms of the letters of Scripture and is graced with an ecstatic vision of the Divine Name: the true and ineffable point of Infinite Plenitude.[10]

And if all this were not enough, yet other mystical hermeneuts—and the tradition goes back to the early centuries of our era—even made the audacious claim that the historical Torah given at Sinai is nothing less than a reflex of inscriptions on the divine cosmic body, as it were, so that a proper penetration of the veils of Scripture will lead to an ecstatic vision of the cosmic form of God, who is actually formed out of Scriptural language—a kind of hieroglyphic hologram! Now such a notion of the ontological uniqueness of Scripture has its roots in the notion that no section or even letter of the Torah is extraneous. Nachmanides, in the thirteenth century, said that this notion was eventually meant to include obscure geographic pericopae and name lists; and his contemporary, R. Azriel of Gerona, even went so far as to say that "there is no [ontological] distinction between [Genesis 36, which deals with] the chiefs of Edom and the Ten Commandments: *for it is all one thing and one structure.*" But see now the absolutely astonishing development of this mystical notion (undoubtedly derived from ecstatic experience), found in a forgotten kabbalistic book called *The Book of [Divine] Unity.* Here we read:

> All the letters of the Torah, in all their shapes—combined and separated; swaddled, curved and crooked ones; superfluous and elliptical letters; minute, and large and inverted ones . . . ; [indeed, even] the calligraphy of the letters, [as well as] the open and closed pericopae, and the [liturgical] subdivisions—*all of them constitute the very shape of God,* Blessed be He. . . . [Therefore,] if [even] one letter were to be deleted from the Torah scroll, or one be added, or a [closed] pericope be [written] in an open fashion . . . [or vice versa]: that Torah scroll is disqualified; *for it no longer has in it the shape of God,* may He be blessed . . . , because of the change the shape caused.[11]

More could be said, but the point is clear enough: Scripture—even its blank spaces—is a kind of icon of divinity for the purpose of envisaging God. But it is also an icon to be broken so that one may spiritually ascend into the imageless life of God. And so for many medieval Jewish mystics, Scripture is the ultimate *Sondersprache:* a word which communicates content and yet fundamentally transcends all such communicability; a word which presents Reality and yet is, at the same time, Reality itself. Perhaps nothing emphasizes this point more than the mystical teaching that even the most apparently irrelevant passage in Scripture is an entry to divine experience. Speaking of Genesis 36 noted earlier, R. Ḥayyim Azulai said that if a person were to spend the entire day reading Gen. 36:22 ("And Lotan's sister was Timna") he could thereby attain mystical bliss; for

> When a man utters words of the Torah, he never ceases to create spiritual potencies and new lights, which issue like medicines from ever new combinations of the elements and consonants. If therefore he spends the whole day reading just this one verse, he attains eternal beatitude, for at all times, indeed, in every moment, the composition [of the inner linguistic elements] changes in accordance with the condition and rank of the moment, and in accordance with the names that flare up within him at this moment.[12]

III

So where do we stand now? It certainly makes considerable difference for any estimation of the ontology or sanctity of Scripture when its language is regarded (as among the ancient rabbis) as a record of the unique will and speech of God; or (as among philosophical and mystical esotericists) when the plain-sense of Torah is compared to several veils—or garments—of meaning leading ultimately to the Meaning of all meaning, to the preternatural divine Reality. In the latter case, the ontological uniqueness and sanctity of Scripture are, quite apart from their functional role in the religious community, fundamentally a verbal link to and a distillate of God. As such, the language of Scripture is both communicable and noncommunicable in any ordinary sense. Indeed, as I have intimated, it is both a glyph and hieroglyph, sense and transcendence at once. In mystical meditations, then, the true *métier* of Scripture is that it is an inscription of infinite profundity, depth, and power—one truly worthy to be called a "Word of God."

Perhaps these remarks may help somewhat to clarify where we now stand, and just how new and different from that of our forebears any contemporary attempt to speak of the sanctity or special ontology of Scripture must be. Before providing one or two hints of my own thinking on this matter, let me bring my discussion of the difficulties into even clearer focus by saying that with the modern period—and let us invoke Spinoza for the purpose—there has been a massive reduction of Scripture as a *Sondersprache* to Scripture as a conditioned language, like any human language. Now in some cases the diminution of the special power of Scriptural language stopped at the half-way house called "aesthetics"; and already in the eighteenth century the vitriol of theological dogmatics was decidedly neutralized through a preoccupation with this comparatively bland common denominator of biblical scholarship. Characteristic of these times is the letter of Moses Mendelssohn to Hofrath Michaelis (who worked on Lowth) about November, 1770:

> I feel certain that you will treat the Psalms as poetry, without regard to the prophetic and mystical which Christian as well as Jewish expositors found in the Psalms only because they looked for them there; and they only looked for them there because they were neither philosophers nor judges of literature.[13]

But all this shilly-shallying about aesthetics aside, the real *Novum Organum* that fully and fatefully shrank the speech of Scripture to the proportions of human language was natural or scientific method. For this method seeks clarity and all-too-human plain-sense; it wants to expose nonsense and obscurantism wherever it may lurk, and thus bring the "ghooolies and ghosties and long-leggity beasties" of language into the light of its "real" maturity. And so, is it any great surprise that our metaphor of concealment and unveiling has gone through a series of ironic and sometimes demonic transformations in a host of Western languages in recent centuries? Among some books that attempted the ultimate exposé, let us recall Knorr von Rosenroth's innovative *Kabbala Denudata,* Eisenmenger's perfidious *Entdecktes Judentums,* and among numerous comparable titles in the eighteenth century, Nicolas Antoine Boulanger's well-known treatment of mythology called *L'Antiquité Dévoilée.* Finally, in our own day, Roland Barthes is perhaps a sign of the times when he compares the task of interpretation to peeling the skin off an onion, since at the end of the process there is nothing left but the will-to-power of the reader/peeler.

Where textual meaning is always produced at will, and not ever found outside the self—at least as an initial provocation, and where the *fascinosum* of literature is not combined with a sense of the mysterious powers revealed in it and by the surplus of meanings conveyed by such powerful texts—in these circumstances one is quite far from anything even remotely resembling the ontology and sanctity of Scripture as it has emerged from our preceding discussion. Might we say, for starters, that "high poetry" and deeply reflexive prose are good candidates in our day to continue the tradition of *Sondersprache*—that is, of a speech which communicates but is also not ordinary discourse because it points to deep surpluses of meaning, and which also releases to the reader or hearer some presentiment of the dark and mysterious forces out of which meanings are constituted? Do not these two literary forms, at their best, bear the twin attributes of a *Sondersprache*—of both proclamation and presence, that is, of the articulation of an image of existence and also its tangible and fragile actualization? . . . Or is all this mere twaddle and a bit of modern idolatry? For is not a *Sondersprache* also a speech that is utterly not human—something akin to the voice of God in the Book of Nature or the Books of Moses in a most distillate form? Along these lines, let me conclude with a final musing and suggest that perhaps the deep core of a *Sondersprache* is just there where voice and being are one, and where this unity is centered in every word and letter—something like "The Aleph" of Borges and of kabbalists of all generations and traditions. Here is an alphabetic prism one might conjure by, and thus be conjured into infinite depths; and here, too, is a *logos* whose disclosure is not aesthetic pleasure but a divine apocalypse—a rending of the garment of heaven. Among moderns, Walter Benjamin understood this well when he remarked that truth is not "an unveiling which destroys the secret, but the revelation which does it justice."[14] Our contemporary search for an "aleph" amid the ruins of old texts and words is part of the modern quest; and we have become like prowlers around Sinai, only momentarily assuaged—at best—by poetic insights. Perhaps for now we must be content with a simple readiness to perceive the disclosure of an "aleph" when it may come—and with it the possibility of a new metaphysics of speech.

·II·

SCRIPTURAL HERMENEUTICS AND THE FORMS OF CULTURE

·4·

ISRAEL AND THE "MOTHERS"

It is sometimes necessary to "go to the Indies," as an old saw has it, to see oneself in perspective. The historical and comparative study of religion has taken this advice with gusto, and the results in our century are a vast revisioning of the structures of religious experience and expression. Poor Dorian Gray, the lens which catches his image is ever-changing. One must therefore be concerned that the cultural configurations reflected by scholarly study adequately approximate the phenomena at hand. And one must ask: are these patterns merely methodological projections which over-assimilate distinct data; or is there real explanatory power in the models used for analysis? Such questions become more acute as the amount of detail diminishes—which is often the case for the religions of Near Eastern antiquity. Frequently, structural polarities which seem productive from one perspective are distorting from quite another; and apparently fundamental differences are often more reconcilable than one may initially think. It is then intriguing to correlate these intersecting structures, and to trace their transformations from one "pure" type to another.

In the following, I aim to reconsider the old and vaunted polarity of ancient Israel and its pagan neighbors. Formally, it would seem, the religious structures of Israel and Canaan are at irreconcilable odds—or so one would conclude from the face-off between Elijah and the prophets of Ba'al. But let us not forget that the prophetic purism of Elijah confronted a popular attitude in which such differences were less menacing. "How long," he demanded, "will you hop between two branches? If the Lord is God, follow him; but if Ba'al [is God], follow him" (I Kings 18:21). One must wonder at the structure of this hopping, and ask how two such branches might stem from one tree? In order to appreciate the dialectics involved, the broad differences between Yahwism and Ba'alism must first be drawn. Since the evidence of Canaanite religion is sparse and scat-

A version of this essay was originally published in *The Other Side of God*, ed. P. Berger (Garden City, N.Y.: Doubleday, 1981), 28–47, and is used here by permission.

tered, this data must be combined with the more amply documented details of other ancient Near Eastern religions.

I

The cumulative evidence of ancient Near Eastern religions presents us with an identifiable mythic structure. By this structure I have in mind a cosmos perceived as a plenum, interlocking and interconnected in substance. This substance is a unity—insofar as nature is perceived as an unbroken continuum pulsating with divine life. Indeed, it is the very power and vitality of the gods which constitutes this chain of natural being. The world is not merely the garment of the gods, it is also their very body and substance. As one distinguished writer on ancient Egypt has ventured to put it: "There was . . . a continuing substance across the phenomena of the universe, whether organic, inorganic, or abstract . . . to the ancient Egyptian the elements of the universe were consubstantial."[1]

And why is this so? One reason is certainly rooted in the intuition that the distinguishable divine powers which make up this world constitute moments of emergence or differentiation from within one primal and inchoate element. Cosmogony is the final result of theogony: first there is the productive and repeated commingling of this divine element until the various gods are born; and then occur the subsequent antagonisms and redistributions of power among these gods from which results the world as we find it. The myths which conceptualize these intuitions differ greatly and cannot be reduced one to the other. In Mesopotamia, theogony and theomachy (as in *Enuma elish*) are often successive features resulting in cosmogony and anthropogony; in Canaan, by contrast, theogonic elements are found in one genre of texts while theomachy and cosmogony appear in others (such as the Baʿal and ʿAnat Cycle); whereas in Egypt emanationist configurations from a primordial godhead sometimes set the pattern of theogony and cosmogony (as in the creation by Atum), and these are generically separate from combats between the resultant gods (such as Horus and Seth).[2] But however these myths differ, they commonly underscore the notion of a cosmic continuum, of a monism of divine life which finds expression or individuation in and through the plenum of nature. Perhaps an old myth about Atum, preserved in the Memphite tradition, best summarizes this matter in its crudely profound way when it refers to the origin of all things in a divine act of masturbation. The gods are the all-in-all; there is nothing which they are not, for their totality is wholeness itself.

In this world view, the gods are immanent and near, and there is a deep harmony linking man and god and world. This harmony is truly ontological. And how could it be otherwise? Do not man, god, and world share the same substance? Is not mankind created out of the very bodies of Tiamiat's cohorts in *Enuma elish*, even as the world is itself carved out of her desiccated hulk? The same energies flow throughout all being; indeed, there is a macrocosmic-microcosmic homology: all is linked, and every level of being ontologically "mirrors" all others. The cosmic *organum* is thus redolent with "sympathies" and correspondencies; an intricate and eternal network of correlations links gods and men, gods and nature, men and nature. Within this mythic monism, man could always say: "I am *also* that."

As S. Giedion has reminded us, in his great studies of prehistoric art and the beginnings of architecture: "Only if we understand the religious conviction that no discrimination was conceivable within the realm of animate matter can we comprehend that an insignificant insect and the cosmic godhead could be one and the same."[3] For, indeed, in ancient Egypt the god of creation (Atum) was identified with a lizard, and the sun-god (Ra) with a dung beetle. The transmutation of deities into animals, and animals into deities, was expressive of the ontological intuition that the bond of life was—for all its diverse manifestations—unbroken. Throughout this ancient world the life forces enlivening the biocosmic continuum were embodied in perceptible forms—the very forms of nature and its processes. And they were also embodied in figures and representations. These images—be they the signata of the sun, the figures of thunder-hurling storm gods such as Baʿal, or the nurturant features of mother goddesses such as Qudshu-Asherah-Astarte—brought to archetypal expression the divine powers which link all realms of existence one to the other: the gods were in and of nature, and so was mankind. The iconic forms of the public and private cults gave concrete representation to the energies embodied in the world. These icons are truly gods and truly their representation.

The divine powers which constitute the depth and breadth of this entire nurturant and sustaining cosmos may be termed "the Mothers"—for all their diverse personifications and genders. And humankind, which has emerged from this engendering body as flesh of its flesh, remains dependent upon it as to the source of life itself. The "sympathies" and homologies between gods, men, and nature are also the sources of human meanings. The unified web of things rendered everything potentially ominous, potentially an omen by which to divine the will of the gods. This will is expressed in the stars and in the planets; in the entrails of sheep and in chance sounds; in the dreams of mankind by night and in their physical monsters by day. Experts studied the occurrences together with their correlations, checked them against events, and deepened their wisdom as to the inner nature of things. Revelation of divine will was thus not independent of "creation" or nature; divine will did not transcend the substance of the natural world. And this was equally true for the relationship between law and nature. In ancient Egypt *ma'at*—the principle of order, harmony, and justice—is a feature in and of the very structure of things. The pharaohs embodied this principle and through their rule and legal dicta humanized it for mankind in society. In ancient Mesopotamia, too, the principles of justice are embedded in the cosmic structure of things. It is the *me* of justice—as general principle—which the god Shamash allows Hammurapi to perceive, and so establish, concretely, *kittu u mesharu* (justice and right) on earth.[4]

But the "sympathies" and homologies between gods-men-nature/world are most fully present in the rhythms of life itself. It is here that the deepest needs and anxieties of humankind are "acted out" and projected onto the nature of things. Let us recall the simple and profound—but so often overlooked—insight of the great photographer F. Sommer, who observed that it is not nature which is "alive" but we who give it life. We animate nature by our personifications of its processes. In the ancient world, too, nature came alive as a pattern of dying and rebirth, of waning and waxing, of disappearance and emergence, and of desiccation and envigoration. The combats between divine forces (Seth and Osiris; Mot and Ba'al), the search for the powers of life (Isis and 'Anat), and the wailing and the celebrations (for Dumuzi; for Ba'al), all gave dramatic expression to what was deeply felt and everywhere seen. The mythic narratives on one level, like the dramatic mimes on another (cf. the *Min* and *Akitu* festivals; or the fertility rituals in Ugaritic texts) sympathetically sought to envigorate the processes of life and death. The waning and waxing of the moon, the cycles of seed time and harvest, the impregnation and gestation of wombs, are all homologies of one another.[5]

Mankind lives in the rhythms of nature, and so ritual expressions (such as the *hieros gamos*, and sacred prostitution, such as the defeat of the forces of disorder and sterility) participate in the cycle of life and help regenerate it. Life and death form an unbroken bond; the body of the underworld god Mot is, in Ugaritic literature, winnowed and enters the earth like seeds for new life. Death, hidden like seeds in the soil, is pregerminative. The substance of nature is one—mankind included. Salvation is cyclical; it is in and through the rhythms of nature. And if mankind is called upon to imitate the gods, and to reiterate their patterns, this is because the biocosmic energy is one; this is because human *eros*, in all its desires and urges, partakes of the *eros* of the gods. Man is made in the image of the gods, and his life is one profound *imitatio dei*. The dramas of ritual only make this explicit and focused in his consciousness.

II

It was against this awesome insight into the teeming vastness and unity of natural life that ancient Israel made its leap of consciousness. The concordance of all-in-all was ruptured; a hierarchy of natural differentiations, separated and ordered in accordance with a supernatural divine will, was spoken in Gen. 1–2:4a. This creation account reflects the mature vision of a new religious orientation. Leo Strauss, in his penetrating essay on Jerusalem and Athens, aptly noted the subtle but marked accent in this document toward a religious anthropology.[6] The focus is on man and man's world; the heavenly bodies serve as time references for human life; plant and animal life are under his domain. There is, then, a shift away from heaven and any divinization of the forces of nature. Elohim is unengendered; there is neither theogony nor combat. Indeed, for all the mythic vestigiality of man made in the image of God,[7] or of a postscript referring to the *toledot* of heaven and earth (2:4a; *toledot* refers literally not to history but to "generation"), there is no panerotic or pandivine aspect to the orderly creation by Elohim. Later psalmists would underscore this vision with their emphasis that creation ever praises God, and that his creative spirit enlivens and nurtures all life (cf. Pss. 104:24–30; 145:10, 16). But such a god is distinct from nature, which neither contains him nor exhausts his power. It is "will" which characterizes such a god. Such a one, says Gerardus van der Leeuw, is a Father—beneficent perhaps—but not a Mother.[8]

Such a religious vision was achieved at a great cost and required a fundamental spiritual transformation. The "great cost" involved is not so much the many remarkable attempts to absorb, reformulate, or otherwise integrate the mythic patterns, images, and values of Canaanite and ancient Near Eastern religions—though they are significant attempts and not to be minimized. The "great cost" is that this cataclysmic *Götterver-nichtung* opened an awesome abyss between God and man-world/nature. Let us not forget in this connection that the monotheistic revolution of ancient Israel—like that of Islam in its own time—is, from the viewpoint of the history of religions, a devolution. The phenomenon of a sky god who is an impartial sovereign and source of all law and order for the world, and who often becomes otiose or is replaced by the youthful vigor of the gods of nature (his sons and children), is widespread and well known. It is, indeed, a phenomenon found in the ancient Near East as well: e.g., Anu is replaced by Enlil; El is replaced by Ba'al. The gods of nature come closer to mankind, and sustain it. Israel reopened the abyss.

The chasm which separated God and man was crossed from two sides: it was crossed by the word of man in prayer and by the will of God in revelation. God's word expressed his will and confronted its recipients with demands: the patriarchs were confronted, Moses was confronted, and so were all the prophets. These prophets were successively addressed by the holy one of Sinai, whose presence and whose will confronted the Israelites in the desert. At Sinai, in fact, a fundamental spiritual transformation occurred: it was now divine will which correlated all the spheres of existence. In the words of later covenantal formulations, obedience was to be blessed with the fruits and fertility of nature, disobedience with drought and a cast-iron sky; blessing brought with it social order and peace, while curse doomed the people to war and exile. All was linked to the condition "If you obey my Commandments" (cf. Deut. 11:13–25; 28:10–69).

No power could be more embracing, no god more omnipotent, than the nameless, imageless God of Israel. No guarantee of the beneficent life of nature could exceed the promises of the covenant, spoken by One who was not seen—cannot be seen. Deut. 4:12–19 drives this point hard in its homily on the imageless god: it takes up the very hierarchy of forms created in Gen. 1:2–4a and denies them all representational equivalence with the Revealer. The Creator and Revealer are one God—who is neither in nor of nature. And so revelation is also not grounded in nature. The source of the Law is supernatural. And yet observance of this Law— and it alone!—guarantees rain in its season.

The fundamental gulf which opens up between this mythos of an omnipotent and transnatural divine will and the created, natural world is thus bridged by the covenant law. But not by this alone. For the divine will also appears within the sphere of human history and transforms it. Now it is true that several Mesopotamian gods do respond to and determine the fate of human history. But history is not a privileged mode of their appearance, insofar as they remain essentially grounded in the natural plenum of things. By contrast, the God of Israel is free of all forms and substances, and remains free to exercise his will however he chooses. And he chooses to do so in history. Indeed, history and time are given new meaning as the expression and mode of manifestation of a god of omnipotent will. Historical time becomes the dimension and record of such a god's activity. Such a modality of time is not linked to natural cycles; it is not cyclical. Indeed, such a modality of time is solely a reflex of an unconditional and unqualified divine will. *Imitatio dei* is thus not the representation or reiteration of primordial acts of the gods which have their eternal reflex in the natural cycle; *imitatio dei* is rather obedience to the divine will and imitation of certain divine attributes (e.g., Exod. 22:24–26).

In the Bible, the category of history also determines the way older natural rhythms are assimilated and relived: the harvest festivals memorialize moments in Israel's historical destiny (they are moments of manifest divine will); the Sabbath is no longer a term designating a moment in the lunar flux, but transcends the natural cycle. The correlation of festivals with the new and full moon is no longer emphasized. Natural bounty becomes occasions for historical credos (cf. Deut. 26); the seasons of life benefit from observance of the law (cf. Deut. 28). The conditional grace of a rewarding Father replaces the unconditioned love of Mother Nature. A new consciousness has clearly set in. God and the gods are not as near or as real as one's body and the earth. The God of Israel is an incomparable god in heaven; but his law can be as near as one's mouth and heart (Deut. 30:11–14). Alienation from nature and from God is overcome by obedience: the law of God mediates and regulates all things.

III

The foregoing discussion would thus serve to pit Cosmos vs. History, the gods of Nature vs. the God of Omnipotent Will, as mutually exclusive religious options. Indeed, official Israelite theology in its various genres—historiography, psalmody, prophecy—is fundamentally rooted in this bifurcation. From the official covenantal perspective, cultic involvement with the gods of the ancient Near East is the arch sin and a central reason for divine wrath and punishment (e.g., Judg. 2:11–23; II Kings 17:7–23). But it is just here that a most fundamental paradox arises, one which bears significantly on the theoretical problem outlined at the outset of this discussion. For side by side with the official historiographies, and in dialectical relation with them, another form of ancient Israelite worship emerges. The apparent contrast between the religions of cosmos and a religion of covenant, between religions in which god, man, and world are fundamentally nondifferentiated—i.e., they partake of the same cosmic "substance"—and the official religion of Israel in which God is wholly other than man-world, is radically contradicted by a fully evidenced and long-enduring syncretism.

The paradox is not that Cosmos vs. History is an improper juxtaposition, but rather that it is most proper. As opposed to the viewpoint most fully articulated in the *later* covenantal theology, in which obedience to the will of the God of Israel will bring on nature's benefits, sources from earliest times suggest a popular discontent with the notion that a transcendent God of history rules nature. Moving from a seminomadic to an agrarian environment, there was the tendency among ancient Israelites to prefer the local nature gods. After all, YHWH had simply not proved himself an agrarian deity. Thus, to whatever degree the divine promises to the patriarchs, or the conquest account itself, were intended to impress the notion of YHWH was the true Land-Lord (Baʿal) of Canaan, many remained unimpressed. From the very first, Israelites were involved in orgiastic fertility rituals (as at Baʿal Peor, Num. 25:1–9) and built altars to Baʿal with sacred trees devoted to Asherah (El's wife) attached thereto (Judg. 6:25, 28, 30). In an ironic touch which underscored the *Kulturkampf* involved, Gideon trampled his father's altar to Baʿal with a young bull—this latter being an old iconic representation of Baʿal's fertile force.

It is one of the peculiarities of official Israelite religious literature that it so insistently preserves the record of national apostasies. All the same, this record provides an invaluable index of the depth and breadth which bull imagery and Canaanite fertility practices infiltrated ancient Israelite religious life. Figures of bulls were set up in the tenth century B.C.E. by Jeroboam at the shrines of Dan and Beth-el (I Kings 12:28 ff.); and two centuries later Hosea still refers to practices associated with them (8:5 f.). The form of the bull is probably a reflection of the belief in some circles that YHWH had absorbed the properties of the Canaanite god El.[9] This would have been one path whereby various Canaanite practices would have found their point of entry into official Israelite worship. Thus pillars to Asherah were even set up in the Temple itself (II Kings 21:3); and official fertility votaries began to appear (I Kings 15:11 f.). An echo of a violent reaction against these practices by the Jerusalemite priesthood may be found in the portrayal of the orgiastic episode connected with the worship of the Golden Calf (Exod. 32), for it has been well observed that the language of this text has been significantly influenced by the depiction of Jeroboam's apostasy.[10] From this perspective a later inner-priestly polemic was anachronistically retrojected into Israel's earlier history. Be the truth of this as it may, the literary juxtaposition of the Sinaitic theophany with the Golden Calf episode is richly symbolic of ongoing tensions and confusions in ancient Israelite religion.

The extent of the syncretism knew no bounds. From early times on, royal circles introduced and sanctioned Canaanite personnel and elements (e.g., I Kings 16:29–34; II Kings 10:18–29), and the people moved back and forth as their religious focus and needs required. Indeed, this is just the point of Elijah's remarks against the people in the ninth century B.C.E.: "How long will you hop between two branches?" The ordeal between Elijah and the prophets of Baʿal portrayed in I Kings 18 was expressly stated as a judgment as to who was the real God: YHWH or Baʿal (v. 21). It seems that most Israelites doubted that YHWH could bring rain, health, and fertility. For well beyond the specific ordeal on Mount Carmel, the various hagiographic legends of Elijah (and his successor Elisha, too) all pivot around such life issues. At one point, in fact, Elijah excoriates King Ahaziah for beseeching the oracle of Baʿal Zebub (god of healing) in his sickness with the words: "Is there no god in Israel that you go to beseech Ba'al Zebub, god of Ekron?" (II Kings 1:3; cf. vv. 6, 16).

Elijah's God, the God of the patriarchs (I Kings 18:36), was in the end victorious and did bring on the rains (vv. 38–45)—despite the ecstatic practices of the prophets of Ba'al and Asherah.[11] But it is the sequel to this event in I Kings 19 which is even more instructive. Fleeing to Mount Horeb as a Moses *redivivus*, Elijah received a theophany from his god.[12] In the depiction of this event the polemic between YHWH and Ba'al, the *numen* in and of the storm, is sharply cast: YHWH, the text says, was not in the storm or the wind; he was not in nor of any of the phenomena of nature (vv. 11–12). YHWH transcended them all. His appearance was but a silent timbre: a paradoxical voiced silence. The God of Israel is not to be identified with the forces of nature, the text implies; and yet nature is responsive to his will, and his alone.

But this protest notwithstanding, the situation in the eighth century B.C.E. was hardly different from the one which preceded it. Nevertheless, several new facets appear and are of interest. In Hos. 4–13 we hear over and over again how the Israelites partook of Canaanite practices. For example, they celebrated and sought to influence the forces of fertility by practicing ritual sex at festival occasions, and on the threshing floor at harvest time (4:14; 9:1–2). In these and a myriad other ways they served Ba'al in Dan and Beth-el. Whether YHWH could bring the bounty of nature seems again at issue. And indeed, it is just this point which is highlighted in Hos. 2:7. The prophet says that the people have forsaken YHWH for Ba'al, not knowing that it is YHWH (who took them out of Egypt, v. 15) who brings this boon (vv. 10–11). In future days the Israelites will not call him "my Lord" (lit., "my Ba'al"), or call on any of the ba'als (vv. 18–19). They will experience a covenant that YHWH will make for them with all of nature (v. 20). For it is he alone who can make nature "respond" with providential fertility (vv. 23–24). (And lest the prophet's pun be lost, let us simply observe that this fertile "responsiveness" of nature is conveyed by a verb playing on the name of the Canaanite fertility goddess 'Anat.[13]) YHWH will be Israel's husband; her former sexual alliances with Ba'al will be replaced by new covenantal vows (vv. 21–22). Israel's ritual dalliance with Ba'al is thus transformed by the imagery of a covenantal marriage. Fertility rites will be replaced by obedience to the divine will. The erotic was sublimated by a covenantal *hieros gamos*.

Syncretistic practices continued throughout the seventh to sixth centuries B.C.E. and continued to cut across official and popular spheres. Thus, e.g., the prophet Jeremiah refers to involvements in Canaanite fertility practices (2:20–25), to oaths to Ba'al (5:7; 12:16) and to prophecies in his name (2:8; 23:13). Doubts as to YHWH's power to bring rain continued to exist, as we can see from cultic statements to the contrary

(Jer. 14:22); and a cult to Ishtar, Queen of Heaven, is referred to (Jer. 7:18), as well as cults to other cosmic powers such as the sun, moon, and zodiac (Jer. 19:13; II Kings 23:5; Zeph. 1:4–5, 8). Ezekiel, Jeremiah's contemporary, also refers to rituals to the sun (8:16) and to Tammuz, the Mesopotamian numen of the grain (8:14). Concern with the powers of fertility is also expressed in the numerous figurines of naked women found in Israelite archaeological strata of this period;[14] and the iconic images of the sun and moon are also represented there.

Lest we assume that these practices had no official standing, let us note that Ezekiel reports icons and pagan rites in the Temple (8:10–12); and during the same period, under royal direction, worship of Ba'al, Asherah, and various astral deities was set up throughout the land and in the Temple precinct itself (II Kings 21:3–7; cf. 23:4–6 and Ezek. 8:4, 16).[15] There were even dormitories for the hierodules in the Temple, "where women wove garments for Asherah" (II Kings 23:7). Accordingly, the contemporary prohibitions in the book of Deuteronomy against setting up an Asherah in the shrine, or receiving a hierodule's fare therein, were based on existing practices (Deut. 16:21; 23:18–19). One can hardly doubt that any of these practices could have existed in the Temple without the support of the official priests of YHWH. Indeed, an explicit reference in this regard may be found in Ezek. 44:6–12.

IV

What are we now to make of these syncretistic products of Israelite and Canaanite religious worship? For does all this evidence not raise fundamental doubts as to whether Yahwism and Ba'alism are mutually exclusive religious configurations? It seems quite evident that the position of religious purism was a restricted ideology at best, even if it was the ideology of those who in fact edited the Hebrew Bible. Nevertheless, it must be stressed that the religious impulses which erupted to create pure Yahwism were truly revolutionary when seen against the mythic structure and stage of development of regional religions of the time. These impulses contained religious intuitions which theoretically drove an impassable wedge between the God of Sinai and the gods of nature. This much is certain.

But it is equally certain that the gulf was crossed—although here our vision is obscured by the dark glass of polemical texts. It is irritatingly unclear just how syncretistic notions developed in ancient Israel and how they were maintained in religious consciousness. Should we say that this syncretism was a paradoxical development and that the new Yahwistic phenomenon sought to absorb the entire plurality of nature gods (as the very divine name Elohim—literally "gods"—suggests)? Did Israel try to integrate fertility gods like Baʿal, and so serve YHWH in some Baʿalistic forms, only to find that these rituals so split their consciousness that they soon served powers other than YHWH, at least for some matters? Or is this prophetic perspective a distortion due to the pressures of purism? Some texts make it appear that the struggle to integrate a high God of Heaven and history with the near gods of nature and cosmos was never quite successful. If this is so, many Israelites must have felt that there were two types of power in heaven: YHWH and the gods of Canaan. Was YHWH considered by such persons just one—albeit favored and with special attributes—god in the pantheon? Was the attempt to portray YHWH as fully transcendent to the cosmic plenum, as ontologically unique, never quite common coin?

We must not shrink from such a possibility, as one often overlooked text makes quite clear. For were it not for Jer. 44, we might assume that Israelite worship of cosmic powers and the like was often nothing but worship of YHWH via natural representations and expressions of his creative power (in much the same way as the iconic image of Phoebus Apollo on the sixth-century C.E. mosaic floor of the Beth Alpha synagogue has been interpreted).[16]

In chapter 44 we find a remarkable clash of explanations among the exiles of Judea. Jeremiah excoriates the exiles for worshiping "other gods" in Egypt when it was for just such practices that YHWH destroyed Jerusalem and the cities of Judea (vv. 1–10). Undaunted, the husbands—who knew their wives to be engaged in cult practices to other gods—the women, and the whole exile in Egypt answered the prophet that when they were in Judea, offering incense to the Queen of Heaven, pouring her libations and baking cakes, all was well. It was only when they ceased, presumably in response to prophetic demands, that she became upset and the ill of exile befell them. They therefore decided to fulfill their vows to the Queen of Heaven and perform her cult service (vv. 15–19, 25).[17] This was in the sixth century B.C.E. A century later the Elephantine papyri indicate that the Queen of Heaven had a temple in Syene, and that Jews swore by a goddess named Anatyahu.[18] In any event, the Judean exile to whom Jeremiah addresses himself clearly believed that the Queen of Heaven was capable of punishing her devotees with exile for ceasing her worship. No more could have been correspondingly said of YHWH, god of the cult of Jerusalem. Is there any reason to assume that these devotees believed YHWH to be differentiated from the natural plenum in a way that the Queen of Heaven was not?

Perhaps the following might be said: The explosion in religious consciousness which produced Yahwism introduced a fundamental split between Israel and the Canaanite religions of nature. Many believed that

YHWH was differentiated from the natural plenum in a way that the gods of Canaan were not. As "other," he confronted man and world and guided them by his transnatural will. Accordingly the religious purists of Israel claimed that Yahwism and Baʿalism were antinomies and not to be homologized. The religious configuration these protagonists of a pure cult evolved was a self-confirming construct; religious experience and the strategies of purism reinforced the differences. But many could not yoke the "Mothers" to the Father's will. As a shadow side, worship of the numina of the cosmos struggled for independent existence. Their Israelite devotees gave them privileged place, so to say, at the right hand of YHWH. For such worshipers, the notion that Yahwism and Baʿalism represented irreconcilable phenomena was not an issue.

Thus, while such hermeneutical categories as differentiation and non-differentiation do provide a valid heuristic for arranging religious phenomena, their value is limited: on the one hand, syncretism is a fact of religious life; on the other, such theoretical distinctions introduce polarities seemingly irreconcilable for the interpreter, but easily harmonized and sustained by the living religious consciousness.

V

The very concrete nature of "pure" Yahwism and "pure" Baʿalism, and the concrete nature of the syncretistic practices which developed, provides an intriguing point of departure for a consideration of later phenomena in the history of religions. For it seems to me that there is considerable truth to the observation that religions often first produce concrete expressions or objectifications of their deepest religious intentions via myths and cult practices, and that it is only at a later point that these intentions recur in spiritualized or interiorized forms.

One of the most arresting images of pure, concrete Yahwism is the throne vision in Ezek. 1. While this theophanic vision is a complex blend of anthropomorphic, theriomorphic, and volcanic imagery, there is nevertheless conveyed, through distancing similes and exalted expressions, a depiction of the most transcendent god, YHWH. The ontological distance between God and man-world is portrayed in all its awesome enormity. The vision confronts Ezekiel with thunderous otherness. It is no surprise, then, to find that the earliest expressions of Jewish mysticism build on this symbolic structure. The differences and relationships within this ancient mysticism need not concern us here. But what is to be noted is that via spiritual exercises and pneumatic exegesis the adept could begin to ascend the infinite and dangerous way to behold the very Throne of YHWH. This mystical transport is highly spiritualized, to be sure; but no matter how interiorized this "ascension" to the "depths" of existence is, there is never any qualification of the absolute transcendence of God. He is not of this world, but is its Creator. Man and God are never, even at the ultimate point of beatific vision and spiritual adhesion, of the same ontological "substance." In this fundamental sense, early throne mysticism preserves the pure theistic dualism of the Hebrew Bible.[19]

The nature religions of ancient Canaan (Syria and Phoenicia) also have an afterlife, taking on new dimensions in the mystery cults of Hellenistic and Roman antiquity. For while these cults carried over mythological and ritual programs from the ancient Orient, they were nevertheless subjected to profound and thoroughgoing spiritual reinterpretations. It is in this form that they provided the setting for personal mysticism. Thus it is that the mythic perception and ritual enactment of the ancient nature cults regarding the biocosmic unity of all things, and the salvific rhythm of the dying and rebirth of natural forms, provide the schema for sacramental mysteries of initiation and spiritual metamorphosis. The liturgical images of the Mithras mystery presented by A. Dieterich provide a particularly graphic illustration of how a series of ritual stages provide the outer skeleton of an interior journey, in which an initiate dies to his old self so as to be reborn as a new person (and indeed much currency was had of the verbal similarity between Greek "to be an initiate" and "to die").[20]

Whether the spiritual metamorphoses in the mystery religions express the inchoate intention and intuition of the old nature cults cannot be known. In any case, these nature religions were subjected to ever deeper spiritualizations, and many were affected by gnosticizing tendencies—a factor which helps account for initiates' concerns with ascensions to a spiritual source, with acosmic apotheosis, and the like. The profound reinterpretation of the old nature myth of Attis (in the Naasene treatise, the works of Porphyry, Sallustius, and the emperor Julianus) is a case in point. Attis, who turns away from the Great Mother toward the nymph, is identified with the Primal Man who falls into matter. After several episodes (including castration), Attis returns to the Mother, an event signifying rebirth and reunion with the divine world.[21] The adept relates all this to himself, so that the nature myth is exegetically sublimated into a framework for spiritual metamorphosis.

I have touched on these matters because the mythological speculations which Gnostics grafted onto archaic nature myths, as well as the more philosophical speculations of Plotinus, share a vision of the cosmos as a great chain of being. All descends out of an absolute spiritual source, so that even the crudest depths of nature are not ontologically differentiated from this source, but rather retain sparks of the original pure light. Nothing would thus seem more fundamentally different than the throne mysticism which developed from "pure" Yahwistic dualism (God and man-world are differentiated), and the mysticism of the "Mysteries," which developed from "pure" Canaanite monism (gods-man-world are not differentiated). And yet, without entering here into matters of historical influences and complex variations, the Jewish Kabbala presents us with a spiritual syncretism of these two mystical forms.

Over and over again we find Kabbalists taking positions on the relationship between the chain of emanations and the Emanator: Are the two consubstantial (no matter how subtly conceived), or is there a fundamental difference between them? Is all one unity—ontologically undifferentiated, while nevertheless differentiated in terms of the hypostases of the divine potencies? Or is there a hidden point of transcendence which is differentiated even from the divine life which fills "all the worlds"? It is quite clear that monistic annihilations of any ontological differentiation would run the risk of pantheism, whereas a theistic dualism would have to struggle with the meaning of the unity of God. Thus, the eruption of myth within mystical Judaism—an eruption which generated a new consubstantial unity among God and man and world through the realm of the divine emanations which filled all realms of existence in the form of a "Cosmic Tree" or Primal Man—could not ignore its own biblical heritage. These polar configurations had to again be syncretized.

The consubstantial nature of the divine world of emanations meant that all levels of existence could be homologized: thus man is a microcosm of the macrocosmic divine life and his ritual acts are of fundamental significance for maintaining its unity. The spiritual unifications which a mystic performs in the depths of his inner life have profound cosmic ramifications for the deepest unity of God. And as the potencies in this macrocosmic divine life are often hypostasized in masculine and feminine terms, a rich erotic symbolism fills the Kabbala. Man could act out and even initiate, at diverse spiritual and physical levels, events of *hieros gamos* within the Godhead. Rituals thus provide the outer structure for profound spiritual transformations, and are, so the Kabbala teaches, profound mysteries.

And, finally, the meaning of Torah undergoes a remarkable transformation within this Kabbalistic framework. Torah is not simply the mediating embodiment of a transcendent divine will; it is rather mystically one with the totality of divine life which fills the universe. Revelation will now not have to cross an ontological abyss between God and man-world; it can occur repeatedly in the very soul of man. Torah is part of, indeed the very fundamental structure of, the cosmic plenum itself (cf. Egyptian *ma'at;* Greek *sophia;* and the like).[22]

We must stop here, for my concern is not to describe the Kabbala but rather to indicate that the ancient *concrete syncretism* of Israel and the

"Mothers" has its later reflex in the *spiritual syncretism* of the Jewish Kabbala. And yet it is a paradox that just this spiritual syncretism may indicate the underlying intention of its earlier, concrete manifestation. I am inclined to suppose that the accommodation of the "Mothers" within biblical monotheism reflects a distinct longing for direct and immediate contact with the primordial sources of divine power which pulse throughout the cosmos; that it reflects a longing to overcome a felt alienation from God's concrete presence—from a god, that is, whose very life might be experienced in the world, and not only his will.

Given the transformative energy of syncretism in the history of religions, and its profound consequences, we may, perhaps, conclude with the following question: Is there a line which a syncretism of originally distinct religious configurations may not cross without changing the most fundamental intentions of the religions involved? Posed thus, it may be productive to consider the question of religious syncretisms, or of composite religious modalities, as a case study of religious oscillations. One religious pattern might absorb another, alien one and yet remain distinct and identifiable to the extent that its primary intentions are not lost and remain dominant. At this level one may find a practical conjunction of what would be regarded, from a theoretical point of view, as mutually exclusive religious modalities. But at the point that a quantitative absorption of the alien patterns changes the qualitative relation between the two religions, so that the originally dominant configuration becomes the recessive one, the originally dominant religion might die. Or this metamorphosis may contribute to the rise of a new religion. Witness the origin of Christianity.

·5·

FROM SCRIBALISM TO RABBINISM:
PERSPECTIVES ON THE
EMERGENCE
OF CLASSICAL JUDAISM

For the historian of religions, the rise and fall of forms, along with concomitant changes in thought and action, evoke basic questions for the periodization of religious history. What, for example, is the measure of a genuine innovation or rupture in cultural formation; and what, by contrast, is the mark of a mere revival or transformation of old patterns? Merely to contemplate these changes, or chart their occurrences, will thus conjure forth a host of methodological goblins sufficient to test the mettle of even the most valiant interpreter.

Similar concerns confront the historian of art, as well. The profound meditations on temporal development in Henri Focillon's *The Life of Forms in Art* come especially to mind in this regard.[1] The subtle precision of his arguments challenge routine judgments and hasty hypotheses alike. Nevertheless, the elusive potential of bold intuitions, like Karl Jasper's speculations on an "Axial Age" in the late first millenium B.C.E., will always intrigue the cultural historian.[2] While focused on a particular moment in world civilization, Jasper's reflections have broader import. They ponder the occurrence of true transformations in history—of decisive conceptual changes, for example, in the relationship between the transcendental (or cosmic) and the mundane (or human) orders of existence.[3] Such axial developments (or breakthroughs) draw in their wake a flotilla of cultural adjustments. Thus shifts between the transcendental and mundane orders elicit correlative shifts in the relations between myth and revelation or between revelation and reason. Diverse patterns of rejection or accommodation result. Invariably, these changes are revealed by the emergence of new types of holy men, sacred texts and ritual behaviors. Comparative analysis further serves to reveal otherwise obscure configurations in particular cultures, and sets the whole within the full framework of intellectual and religious history.

In the previous chapter, I considered several aspects of axial developments in ancient Israelite religion in connection with its primary break (both conceptual and symbolic) from what I there called the mythic plenum.[4] As I indicated, this formative rupture was neither final nor complete, and different patterns of mythic retrieval are discernable in later Jewish thought. Nevertheless, a decisive dissociation from mythopoeic forms set Israelite religion on an entirely new course. In the present essay I aim to continue this line of analysis and focus on what may be termed a "secondary breakthrough" in ancient Israelite religious history. In brief, my concern is to capture something of the axial transformations that mark the onset of classical Judaism. This involves marking the movement from a culture based on direct divine revelations to one based on their study and reinterpretation. The principal custodians of the former were the sage-scribes of ancient Israel; the purveyors of the latter, the sage-scholars of early Judaism. For their part, the sage-scribes inscribed divine words and traditions as they came to hand. The sage-scholars, on the other hand, variously extended these divine words and sacred traditions through interpretation. To be sure, these scholars inherited modes of study and interpretation from their forebears; at the same time, they also initiated a new centrality and significance for these modes which is nothing short of decisive—and marks the closure of "ancient Israel" and the onset of "ancient Judaism." It is this cultural arc and transformation that my title ("From Scribalism to Rabbinism") strains to signify.

I

The historical records of the early post-exilic period in ancient Israel have left incontrovertible evidence for the reconstruction of our topic. Two details mentioned in connection with Ezra's return from Babylon in the fifth century B.C.E. are especially pertinent. The first is the almost offhand archival notice concerning the loss of the *urim* and *tummim*, the ancient priestly devices for mantic practice (Neh. 7:65). The second is the rather explicit account of a national convocation in the year 458 B.C.E., at which time Ezra led the people in a public event of Torah instruction (Neh. 8:1–8). Together, these facts signal a shift in the modes of access to divine revelation.

Of central importance is the depiction of Ezra himself. As leader of a delegation of returnees to Zion, he is identified as a priest (Ezra 7:1–5) and called "a diligent scribe in the Torah of Moses, which YHWH, God of

Israel, had given" (v. 6), "a scribe of the words of the commandments of YHWH, and His laws for Israel" (v. 11). Ezra is thus, first and foremost, an authoritative guardian of the written revelations. But he is also a teacher of these divine instructions, for we are told that "Ezra set his heart to investigate (*li-drosh*) the Torah of YHWH, and to do and teach [both] law and ordinance in Israel" (v. 10). This is no mere depiction of a routine priestly function of ritual instruction, in the manner of some older pentateuchal accounts (cf. Lev. 10:11). It is, rather, an extension and virtual transformation of this role. Special significance thus lies in the fact that the very idiom used to describe Ezra's activity ("*li-drosh* the Torah of YHWH") is a precise reworking of an ancient formula used to indicate oracular activity (cf. "to consult (*li-drosh*) YHWH," 1 Kings 22:8). Since Ezra's textual task is to seek from the Torah new divine teachings (or explication of older ones) for the present, there is a sense in which exegetical praxis has functionally co-opted older mantic techniques of divine inquiry. This somewhat mantic or inspired dimension of study is underscored by the fact that, in this very context, Ezra is twice described as one who has the "hand of YHWH . . . upon him" (vv. 6, 9). Since early times, this expression was a standard way of denoting the force of divine inspiration upon an individual (cf. Ezek. 1:3).[5]

The combination of these two factors—the resignification of the verb *li-drosh* and the reuse of the idiom 'hand of YHWH'—highlights the chief *novum* of this historical record: Ezra is a priestly scribe who teaches the received, written revelation through his inspired study of it. In the process, the Torah traditions undergo a corresponding refiguration. No dead letter, the ancient divine words become the very means of new instruction through their proper inquiry and interpretation. Ezra is further aided in his task by Levitical instructors who bring Torah understanding (*mebinim*) to the people (Neh. 8:7, 9) and convey to them the sense (*sekel*) of the text being studied (v. 8; cf. v. 13, *le-haskil*).[6] No further indication of inspired interpretation are applied to these teachers. For this dimension, one must turn to Ps. 119:18.

Psalm 119 is a post-exilic prayer replete with Torah piety. The psalmist repeatedly requests instruction in the *received* laws (vv. 12, 27, 33, 64, 66, 68, 73, 108, 124) and, on one occasion, even uses the ancient priestly benediction as a vehicle for petitioning divine grace to guide his understanding of the ancient statutes (v. 135).[7] Elsewhere, he prays: "*gal ʿenay ve-ʾabiṭah nipla'ot mi-toratekha* (unveil [Thou] my eyes that I may behold wonderful things *from out of* Your Torah)" (v. 18). In light of the preceding requests, this plea for illumined visions must also be understood as a petition for divine aid in the interpretation of Scripture.[8] In fact, this request is formulated through a reuse of older mantic terminology— specifically, language known from the traditions of Balaam the seer.

Concerning him we read that "YHWH unveiled the eyes of Balaam, and he saw . . . , (*va-yigal YHWH et ʿeney Bileʿam*) (Num. 22:31). A comparable, contemporary instance marking the transformation of Torah learning occurs in the teachings of Ben Sira. On the one hand, this sage harks back to the terminology of Ezra 7 when he refers to the interpreter of Torah (*doresh ha-torah;* 3:15) as one who "pours out teachings as prophecy" (Eccles. 24:33). At the same time, an echo of the mantic terminology of Ps. 119:18 can also be detected in his admonishment that "many are the mercies of God and He reveals (*yigleh*) His secret to the humble. Search not for what is too wondrous for you (*pilaʾot mimmekha al tidrosh*) and investigate not what is hidden from you. Meditate upon what is permitted to you, and deal not with secret things" (3:20–22).

Both the immediate context of this admonition, as well as early rabbinic citations and discussions of it,[9] suggest that the sage is advised to focus his interpretive skill on the revealed Torah and not to speculate on cosmological or related wonders (*pilaʾot*)—as had become fashionable during the Hellenistic period. Indeed, if he is properly pious, this sage may even hope to receive exegetical revelations (*yigleh*) from God. In this way he is the direct spiritual descendent of the psalmist, cited earlier, who also hoped to receive exegetical revelations (*gal*) from God in order to know the wonders (*niplaʾot*) hidden in the Torah. Both men presuppose a new sensibility: one in which Scripture has become the vehicle of new revelations, and exegesis the means of new access to the divine will. Thus, complementing the divine revelation now embodied in a written Torah, the sage seeks from God the grace of an *ongoing revelation* through the words of Scripture itself—as mediated *through exegesis.*

II

Alongside the "Law," there are the "Prophets" as well. It is therefore of interest to note a parallel development toward the inspired exegesis of written revelations in the prophetic genre as well. As Ezra exemplified the axial shift with respect to the Torah, so Daniel may serve as a paradigm with respect to the prophets. Similar terms for exegetical illumination reinforce this correlation.

It is well known that the traditions about Daniel range from the depiction of a court sage to the purveyor of mantic wisdom. In the oldest records, he and his fellow advisors in the Babylonian court are described as "knowledgable (*maskilim*) in every wisdom . . . and understanders (*mebiney*) of [all] knowledge (*maddaʿ*)" (Dan. 1:4). These abilities include skill in the interpretation of dreams. However, Daniel's role as a latter-day Joseph is decisively altered in the final chapters of the book (Dan. 9–12).

He is there portrayed as inspired with the true meaning of ancient prophecies—prophecies which he reads and studies to small avail until he merits divine guidance. Thus he reports how "I studied (*binoti*) the books" of prophecies in the hopes of knowing the true meaning of Jeremiah's prophecy of seventy years of desolation for Jerusalem (Jer. 25:9–11).[10] It would even appear that Daniel's study was connected with types of ascetic practice designed to achieve this very illumination. For in the immediate context of his study, Daniel reports how he engaged in intense prayer, fasting, and abasement (9:3)—and only then, *in the very course* of these acts (vv. 20–21a), was he granted a vision of the angel Gabriel flying toward him with the words: "Daniel, I have now come forth to give you understanding (*le-haskilekha binah*)" (vv. 21b–22) about the text *he had just been studying* (vv. 24–25). The likelihood that Daniel was engaged in a ritual praxis for exegetical illumination is reinforced by the words of Gabriel himself, who says (v. 23): "At the beginning of your supplication the word (*dabar;* viz., interpretation) came forth, and I have come to tell you that you have found [divine] favor and [are graced with] the understanding of the word (*u-bin ba-dabar*)."[11]

The axial significance of this description of textual illumination is underscored by the narrator's reuse of an ancient literary convention used to present prophetic commissions. This form now serves to legitimate a receiver of exegetical truth *about* the older prophecies. Thus whereas it was earlier reported that a divine being flew (*va-ya'aph*) toward Isaiah and touched (*naga'*) him on the mouth (Isa. 6:6–7), thereby consecrating him to prophecy, we are now told that a divine messenger (an *angelus interpres,* in fact) flew (*mu'aph bi-'aph*) toward Daniel in his vision and touched (*noge'a*) him, thereby initiating him into sealed mysteries of older prophecies. If in the first case the inaugural event occurs as part of an ecstasy induced by the awesome holiness of shrinal practice, and results in a commission to speak the living prophetic word, in the case of Daniel the initiation occurs within an ecstatic trance induced by ritual ceremonies in the context of study. The result is no living word but an interpretation of written oracles. Direct prophecy has ceased here, and is replaced by a knowledge of past texts and their resignification for the future.

Given the importance of this transformation, a second instance of the reuse of prophetic commissions may be noted. In this case, traditions from the book of Ezekiel influence the formulation. One will recall that this prophet had an inaugural vision of the Divine Throne and its fiery panoply while in Babylon, on the banks of the Chebar canal (Ezek. 1:3ff). The vision is described in rich detail—starting with the lower complexes of the chariot and climaxing with a vision of one "like a man" enthroned high above and surrounded by flashes of fire and light (vv. 26–27). Upon seeing this spectacle, the prophet is unloosed by fear (1:1). He is forthwith supported by God and told not to fear (2:6). Indeed, to counteract his fear of incompetence, the prophet is given to eat the very divine words he must proclaim (2:8–3:2). It is perhaps not insignificant for our understanding of late biblical religion that these words are themselves written on a scroll. At any rate, these events conclude with another divine vision and a command that the prophet remain silent (*ve-ne'elamta*) until the Lord will again open his mouth to prophesy (vv. 25–27).

The features from Ezekiel 1–3, together with the already noted characteristics from Isaiah 6, are reworked in Daniel 10.[12] As in Dan. 9:3, this text also begins with a portrayal of Daniel engaged in intense ascetic practices geared to invoking divine illumination. But now, following the example of Ezekiel, Daniel also receives his vision near a bank of water in Babylon (10:4). Moreover, in his trance, Daniel envisages a heavenly figure, of fiery and flashing visage, and falls to the ground in terror (v. 9). The being then raises Daniel up, and tells him that his supplication is accepted and (exegetical) understanding (of the Jeremian oracle) will be granted him (vv. 11–12, 14). Hearing this, Daniel falls dumb (*ne'elamti;* v. 15) and shudders until the divine being tells him not to fear. Then one "like a man" touches (*va-yiga'*) Daniel (v. 18) and tells him that he will be instructed in the meaning of the prophecies that are "inscribed in a true writing" (v. 21). This instruction is found in Daniel 11—a text saturated with reworked passages from the pre-exilic prophets.

Ecstasy induced in conjunction with the study of old prophecies has thus produced a new type of "prophetic" figure—a pneumatic exegete, guided by divine instruction into the true meaning of ancient oracles. Exegetical revelation has thus replaced the radical *novum* of unmediated divine communication to a prophet. At the same time, such exegetical illumination has become a new mode of access to God for a new type of community—formed around teachers and the texts which they authoritatively interpret. This was the earlier situation with Ezra, too, where the reconstitution of the people around Torah study led to formulations of the true community *on the basis of* exegesis performed by authoritative leaders (cf. Ezra 9; Neh. 10). In the case of Daniel, a specific community of interpretation likewise formed. Those in possession of the special exegetical illumination are called "knowers" (*maskilim*) who "understand" (*yabinu*) the true application of the prophecies (12:10; cf. 11:33, 35). Like the students of the Law, whose textual inquiry was guided by God and for whom exegesis had become a mode of divine encounter, the illuminates of Prophecy are also divinely guided into the "hidden and sealed" meanings of ancient revelation (Dan. 12:9). It is this special understanding which functions for them as a mode of divine sustenance in the awesome and wondrous (*pila'ot*) times of the End (v. 6).

III

Textual strands from late biblical literature may further nuance these observations of axial developments in ancient Israelite religious sensibility. If, on the one hand, the emergence of a scriptural corpus of revelations fostered new modes of access to God's will, a more mediated access to divine instruction developed through the exegetical study of the Torah and the Prophets. Such exegetical study contributed to new modes of religious experience. Both features develop and reinforce one another along the trajectory "from scribalism to rabbinism."

The increased importance of the Torah as a corpus of covenantal instructions in the post-exilic community is indicated by many factors. Among these is the reuse of old historical notices in order to emphasize the legal piety of bygone kings. For example, the report referring to Asa's campaigns against cultic abominations (1 Kings 15:11–13) was taken over by the Chronicler (2 Chron. 14:1–2, 4) and supplemented by the comment that the king "obeyed the Torah and commandments" (v. 3). In other instances, the pivotal role of obedience to the Law is introduced into the narrative. A case in point is Solomon's revision of the unconditional promise of divine grace to David (2 Sam. 7:15–16); for in his formulation of it that old divine promise was made conditional upon proper fulfillment of the Law ("no one who will sit on the throne of Israel will be cut off from Me *if* your sons heed their ways, to go before Me as you went before Me"; 1 Kings 8:25). And in a further reappropriation, this transformation was itself reworked in 2 Chron. 6:16. Not content to say that future kings will "go before Me," the Chronicler rewrote the older passage to read "to go *in My Torah* as you went before Me." In this way, the mediating position of the Torah as the condition of dynastic continuity was underscored.

This attitude toward the Torah also affects the nature and expression of religious experience. A comparison of parallel formulations bears this out. The one type, found in a host of liturgical expressions, reflects concrete hopes for divine nearness and help; the other, principally preserved in Psalm 119, reformulates these desires in accordance with its ideology of the Law and commandments. Thus whereas some psalmists say "I have set YHWH (*shivviti YHWH*) before Me" (Ps. 16:8) or urge Israel to "trust in YHWH" (*betaḥ ba-YHWH;* 115:9), the author of Psalm 119 proclaims "I have set your ordinances (*shivviti mishpatekha*) [before me]" (v. 30) and avers that "I have trusted in your word (*bataḥti bi-debarekha*)" (v. 42). Along the same lines, a threnodist exhorts the needy to "Raise your hands (*se'iy . . . kappekha*) to Him (*'elav;* viz., to God)" (Lam. 2:19) in entreaty, while the psalmist piously proclaims that: "I have raised my hands (*va'essa' kappay*) to your commandments (*el mitzvotekha*)" (Ps. 119:48). And finally, we read in Deut. 4:4 of those "who cleave to YHWH (*ha-debeqim ba-YHWH*)," whereas the late psalmist says "I have cleaved to Your testimonies (*dabaqti be-ʿedotekha*)" (v. 31).

These expressions of religious ideology and experience in Psalm 119 must not be assumed to reflect a simple or exclusionary development. Certainly a religious relationship to the Law never supplanted a direct relationship to God. The remarkable clustering of expressions of trust in the Law found in Psalm 119 must rather be attributed to the intense preoccupation of that psalmist with the Torah. In fact, given the fact that this psalm is manifestly an address *to God*, it is reasonable to interpret these expressions of cleaving to the Law or trust in the legal instructions as various attempts by the psalmist to proclaim his consummate loyalty to God's Torah. This granted, it is nevertheless clear that Psalm 119 registers a profound shift of religious sensibility: a deepening of religious experience *in and through* the Torah study. It is only within this framework, I think, that one can properly measure such startling expressions as "I have believed (or relied upon) Your commandments (*be-mitzvotekha he'emanti*)" (Ps. 119:66). The echo of an earlier expression of faith, "And when the Israelites experienced the might which YHWH had wrought in Egypt . . . they believed in YHWH (*va-ya'aminu ba-YHWH*)" (Exod. 14:31), resounds over these late words and counterpoints the momentous developments in ancient Israelite religious life taking place in the post-exilic age.

IV

Alongside the Law as a primary religious modality, similar trends occur with respect to Prophecy. Of particular interest is a striking revision of an old exhortation by the prophet Isaiah (eighth century B.C.E.). Speaking to King Ahaz during the Syro-Ephraimite aggression, the prophet used old military formulae to encourage the monarch to stand firm. "Do not fear," he exhorted, "and let your heart not weaken" (7:4), for YHWH would not allow the invasion to occur. And then, as a capstone to this charge, he added this spiritual condition: "If you do not believe (*ta'aminu;* viz., have reliance) you will not endure (*te'amenu*)" (v. 9b). The overt intent of this exhortation was to promote trust in YHWH's power; and just this was how the Chronicler understood the idiom centuries later. In connection with a military build-up threatening King Jehoshaphat, the king is told: "Do not fear and be not afraid . . . [for] YHWH will be with you" (2 Chron. 20:15, 17); and after this prophetic exhortation Jehoshaphat himself admonished his people with the words: "Believe (*ha'aminu*) in YHWH, your God, and you will endure (*ve-te'amenu*)" (v. 20). But this is not all. After a reprise of the old words of Isaiah, the historian has the king voice this charge: "Believe (*ha'aminu*) *in His prophets* and succeed!" It is thus not solely reliance upon God which will bring salvation and victory; the people must trust in His spokesmen as well.

It would be unwarranted to infer from this historiographical formulation that the Chronicler advocates trust or belief in the prophets (and their oracles) independent of God. The explicit words "believe in *His* prophets" contradict such an inference, and underscore the presentation of the prophet as a messenger of God. Nevertheless, the Chronicler's supplementation of Isaiah's language suggests something more: that the prophets have come to represent intermediary figures who serve an exemplary function for the community. At a time when the prophetic traditions were being gathered, it is significant that several strands of post-exilic historiography recall the prophetic watchword as God's providential interventions on behalf of His people.[13] Failure to heed these warnings of repentance resulted in exile. The Chronicler himself repeatedly presents prophetic words as pivotal in the nation's fate.[14] One may therefore consider his admonition in 2 Chron. 20:20 as indicative of this overall concern.

Parallel to developments in religious experience due to study of the Law, then, the knowledge and study of written prophecies also came to sponsor correlative modes of religious experience. Traces of this development may be discerned by tracking reuses of the verb *ḥakkeh* over six centuries. This verb is used in the prophetic corpus to indicate the act of awaiting the fulfillment of prophecies. Three passages are decisive. The first is Isa. 8:17, where the prophet Isaiah says: "So I shall wait for YHWH (*ḥikkiti la-YHWH*) who is hiding His face from the House of Jacob, and I shall trust in Him." This proclamation of hope concludes a series of oracles dealing with the Assyrian menace, and follows an instruction by the prophet to "seal (*ḥatom*) the oracle" of hope among his disciples (v. 16). His purpose was presumably to preserve a record of the divine words, and thus to dramatize their eventual fulfillment. In the interim, the prophet avers that he will await the Lord—the speaker and fulfiller of these promises. His proclamation is thus entirely different from Hab. 2:3, where the prophet Habakkuk is told by God to write down an oracle of future salvation (vv. 2–3a). An exhortation acknowledging the delayed fulfillment of divine salvation follows this command: "though it tarries, wait (*ḥakkeh*) for it; for it will surely come, without delay" (v. 3b). Note that the formulation here is to "wait for *it*," that is, for the prophecy's fulfillment—and not for God, the fulfiller of prophecies. Accordingly, the famous passage which immediately follows this exhortation, *ve-tzaddiq be-'emunato yiḥyeh*, must surely mean: "and the righteous one will be sustained [rewarded with life] through his faith in *it*." Faithful waiting for the fulfillment of a (written) oracle is thus the life testimony of the *tzaddiq*, the righteous one who trusts God's words.[15]

With this formulation of faithful living with prophecies in mind, we can see how old oracles could be interiorized as a dimension of religious experience. One need not conclude that this religious sensibility is original to Habakkuk in order to sense that, in his articulation of it, a shift has taken place. The full measure of this shift is most fully apparent in Daniel 11–12, where both prophetic passages are reused. Thus Habakkuk's prophecy that salvation will "yet" come (Hab. 2:3a) is cited in Dan. 11:27 and 35; Isaiah's notice (Isa. 8:17) that a prophecy has been "sealed" up among disciples recurs in Dan. 12:4, where the angel Michael instructs Daniel to "seal" (*ḥatom*) the prophecies for the illuminates (cf. v. 9); and the two references to "waiting" for the fulfillment of prophecies are resumed in Daniel's concluding exhortation: "Happy is the one who waits (*ha-meḥakkeh*) and it arrives after 1,345 days" (12:12). Clearly, the faithful waiting for the fulfillment of prophecies is inextricable from the special knowledge which the illuminates (*maskilim*) believe themselves to possess—a knowledge which sustains them during their suffering (11:35; 12:9–10). To be faithful to and believe in the prophecies is thus to believe in their interpretation as mediated by an angelic revelation. It is a situation in which exegesis constitutes the very structure of the religious experience. The result is not so much an expression of emergent "rabbinism" as a mode of "religious scribalism" in one of its remarkable transformations.

V

The various trends discussed so far are continued in the literature of the Dead Sea Scrolls and the early Pharisaic sages. For these two communities, the Law and the Prophets constitute literary collections of revelation; and the ongoing interpretation of these divine words, by authoritative teachers, resulted in an ongoing renewal of revelation and the types of religious experience based upon it. I shall adduce here but the tiniest fragment of this evidence—and even then my concern will be to echo or extend motifs and texts considered earlier. As in the earlier discussions, the axial transformations effected by the interpretation of scriptures will be demonstrated through texts which themselves reinterpret earlier passages from the Bible.

For the sectarian community which produced the Dead Sea Scrolls, the Torah of Moses was their special possession—not because they alone possessed this text, but because they regarded their interpretation of it to be the *only* true interpretation: a special revelation of "hidden things" (*nistarot*) vouchsafed to them through their founding master, the Teacher of Righteousness. Indeed, it was just this special knowledge (*da'at*) of the

Torah which was believed to guarantee salvation to the members of the sect; and it was also this special knowledge which separated them from the community of Israel as a whole—whose oft-proclaimed "evil way" was essentially a *different* interpretation of Scripture. Thus transgression was not so much a rejection of God and His teachings *per se*, as in the rebuke of the prophet Zephaniah against those "who fall away from YHWH and do not beseech Him or seek Him (*derashuhu*)" (1:6). It was much more a rejection of the proper interpretation of that teaching, as is explicitly stated in a passage from the community's *Rule Scroll* (V.11) which transforms Zephaniah's rebuke to say: "the people of iniquity [are those] who walk in the evil way, for they do not beseech [God] and do not seek Him (*derasuhu*) through his laws to know (*la-da'at*) the hidden things (*nistarot*)."

As possessors of these exegetical secrets, both the community and its teacher could say: "These things I know (*yada'ti*) from Your knowledge (*binatekha*), for You have unveiled (*galita*) my ear to mysterious wonders (*raze pela'*)."[16] Surely just this ideological framework illumines the full polemical force of Ben Sira's admonition, cited earlier: "Do not seek out (*tidrosh*) things too wondrous (*pela'ot*) for you . . . ; [but rather] know well (*hitbonen*) what has been permitted to you, and do not deal with hidden things (*nistarot*)." It also sharpens the edge of an old *logion* transmitted in the name of Rabbi Eleazar Ha-Moda'i: "Whosoever desecrates holy things, or contemns the festival seasons, *or reveals* (*megalleh*) *the interior sense* (panim) *of the Torah,* or breaks his convenant with Abraham, our Father, or shames his colleague—though he has [accumulated the merit of] good deeds, he has no share in the World to Come" (*M. Avot* III.11).[17] While diverse, a strong emphasis of this admonition is the concern with ritual offenses (including failure to perform circumcision, which is the "covenant of Abraham" in rabbinic parlance) and inappropriate demeanor (including improper performance of the ritual praxis of study). Accordingly, the sharp censure of those who reveal improperly the deeper sense of Scripture must be understood as directed against those who interpret the Torah "against the *halakha*," as a later glosser of this mishnah has it[18]—which is to say, against the official rabbinic modes of exegesis. Numerous early debates on fixing the festival seasons among early Jewish groups (including strong polemical riposts within the Dead Sea Scrolls themselves), give ample background to the first part of Rabbi Eleazar's teaching. The contemporary rejection of ritual circumcision in Pauline exegesis (Rom. 2:28–29) suggests that this *logion* also has an anti-Christian component.[19] As Paul was at pains to preach, and the sages believed as well, proper exegesis has a salvific dimension. Whoever interprets Scripture incorrectly "has no share in the World to Come."

On route "from scribalism to rabbinism," exegesis thus makes the decisive claim that it is the very means for redemption. And what holds for the Law holds for the Prophets as well. Indicative of this in the literature of Qumran is the remarkable interpretation given to Hab. 2:3. Convinced that the Teacher of Righteousness (*tzedeq*) was pneumatically graced with the *true* understanding of the ancient prophecies, and thus even exceeded what the original prophets understood about the application of their words (*pesher Habakkuk* VII.2), the biblical passage is construed with reference to the sectarian community. Just they, "who [properly] observe the Law," "will God save from the House of Judgment—on account of their tribulation and *their faith in* the Teacher of Righteousness" (VIII. 1–3). Such faith "in" the teacher is, of course, faith in him as a divinely guided medium of "all the mysteries (*razey*) of the words of . . . the prophets" (VII.5)—"for the mysteries of God (*razey 'el*) are wondrous (*le-hapleh*)" (VII.7). The Teacher is thus the revealer of the true meaning of the Law and the Prophets; and knowledge of both is redemptive. Proper practice of the Law does not obviate prophetic hope in the End-time, nor does the proper understanding of the Prophets cancel practice of the Law. The Law is to be observed while one waits for the final days. Thus, when interpreting the passage from Habakkuk that "it will surely come" and one must "wait for it," the sectarians taught: "The interpretation [of it] concerns the men of truth, those who observe the Law, whose hands do not grow slack in the service of the truth, when the last End-time is drawn out for them, for all of God's End-times will come according to their fixed order, as he [the Teacher] decreed for them in the mysteries of his prudence" (VII.10–14).

It was presumably from fear that observance of the Law could be abrogated by prophetic enthusiasts that a final coda was added to the prophetic corpus of Scripture: "Remember the Torah of Moses, My servant, to whom I commanded at Horeb laws and statutes for all Israel" (Mal. 3:22).[20] And it was presumably the revolutionary and antinomian potential of prophecy that induced the early sages to proclaim, despite evidence to the contrary,[21] that "When the last prophets, Haggai, Zechariah, and Malachi died, the holy spirit departed from Israel" (*Tosefta Sota*, XIII.2). A similar concern recurs in the remark that "Since the day when the [first] Temple was destroyed prophecy has been taken from the prophets and given to the sages" (*b. Megillah* 17b). It has been wondered whether such comments derive from anti-Christian concerns.[22] However this be, the strong emphasis in the latter statement on the replacement of prophecy by Torah study provides an instructive foil to the depictions of Ezra and Ben Sira. It will be recalled that both sage-scribes were described with prophetic terminology. Against the background of the foregoing rabbinic *logia*, such depictions seem to express a neutralization of the prophetic impulse—its scribalization, one might say, and its reemployment in the service of the Law.

VI

By way of conclusion, we may recapitulate the range of religious transformations discussed so far through the prism of the image of the Font of Waters, or Well. Among the Dead Sea Scrolls, this image plays a central role in the *Damascus Document* (*CD*). It occurs in the context of an account of the community's origin and its distinctive method of Torah study under the inspired leadership of the Teacher of Righteousness. The scriptural vehicle for this presentation is the so-called Song of the Well (Num. 21:17b–18)—a poetic evocation which "Israel sang" when they stopped for water at a desert oasis called Be'er (Well):

> Spring up, O well!—(Greet it with song):
> The well which the chieftains dug,
> Which the leaders of the people opened up
> With the staff and their maces.

In a precise, atomizing way, the components of this biblical unit are serially resignified: "the Well (*be'er*) is the Law" (*CD* VI.4); "the Staff (*meḥoqqeq*) is the Searcher (*doresh*) of the Law" (VI.7); and "the Leaders of the People" are they who have come to dig the well with the staffs which "the Staff (*meḥoqqeq*) instituted (*ḥaqaq*) to walk in them during all the Epoch of Wickedness" (VI.8–10).[23] Thus in the self-understanding of the community, a new well of Torah has been opened up "with the Staff," this being the Teacher of Righteousness. This new well is, in fact, the source of the secret interpretations (*nistarot*) of the Torah which God Himself "has opened for them; and they [the faithful] digged a well for much water, and whosoever despises it [the water of Torah, correctly understood] shall not live" (*CD* III.14–17). Accordingly, the follower of this way believes himself sustained by the fountain of True Life (the Law) and exults: "I sha[ll praise Thee, My Lord, for Yo]u have placed me at the Font of streams in dry land" (*1Q Hodayot* VIII.4). A more personal testimony of this conviction is expressed by the community psalmist, who says: "Secret Truth You [God] have established in my heart; and Well Water for those who seek it (*doresheha*)" (V.9). Knowledge of the mysteries of the Torah is thus a religious experience: a source of spiritual sustenance in this life and a guarantee of salvation in the Judgment to Come.[24]

The Torah is also deemed the saving water of life in early rabbinic sources. Thus an old Tannaitic tradition allegorically interpreted the reference to "water" in Exod. 15:22 as "Torah" (*b. Baba Qama* 82a). In other instances, directly continuous with the Dead Sea Scroll traditions just cited, scholars of the Law are described as a font of waters. Rabbi Eleazar ben Arak (a student of Rabbi Yoḥanan ben Zakkai) was especially famous for this attribution. For example, in *M. Avot* II.8 he is summarily called "an overflowing fountain"; whereas in the more expanded formulation of *Avot de-Rabbi Nathan* (A) I.14 he is called "a rushing stream, an overflowing fountain—whose waters overflow and go outwards, to fulfill what is stated [in Scripture]: 'Let your fountains burst outward, your rushets of water into the broad places'" (Prov. 5:16). At one level, this characterization of Rabbi Eleazar expresses the boundless learning of a sage; and the choice of Prov. 5:16 as a prooftext also highlights the value of pedagogy so dear to the Tannaitic sages (cf. *Sifrei Deuteronomy* 48). At the same time, one senses that this pedagogical elaboration somewhat neutralizes (or socializes) the image. It is therefore instructive to note another (contemporary) instance of this literary *topos* that focuses on the supernatural boon of Torah study. According to Rabbi Meir in *M. Avot* VI.1, inspired wisdom is one of the divine graces granted the devoted student of the Law. He teaches:

> Whoever devotedly studies the Torah for its own sake merits many things; and not only this but [one may even say] that the entire world is found deserving for his sake. He is called Beloved Companion, who loves the Divine Presence and loves all creatures, [and] who makes the Divine Presence glad and makes glad all creatures. And it [Torah study] robes him with humility and fear; enables him to be righteous, pious, upright and faithful; and keeps him far from sin and near to merit. And people shall benefit from his counsel, discernment, understanding and fortitude . . . *and the mysteries* (razei) *of the Torah are revealed* (megallin) *to him, and he becomes like an overflowing fountain and ceaseless torrent . . . ;* and it makes him great and lifts him above the entire creation.

This teaching permits a deeper glimpse into the spiritual sensibilities of the sages, and their belief in the transformative powers of devoted study. For them, God's manifold grace flows to those sincerely occupied with Torah—who study it without precondition or presumption. Such pure study is divinely requited by gifts of humility and piety, sage counsel and righteousness, and insights into the very mysteries of the Law. Such a person can only be called a Beloved Companion, a friend of God and all creatures. To him is revealed a revelation from the very depths of the Revelation, the written Torah. Devoted study of God's Word thus opens up for him the flood of divine Wisdom, so that he, in turn, may become a font of divine teachings. It is therefore quite likely that this profound religious experience, *of transcendence in and through study,* is also a moment of mystical illumination.[25] One may assume that it was personally known to Rabbi Meir, and that these qualities of an illuminate-sage attracted him to Rabbi Akiva—his student, and himself a reknowned mystic.[26]

Rabbi Meir's *logion* of moral and spiritual transcendence through Torah study is complemented at the end of the next mishnah (VI.2) by a brief teaching in the same style. R. Joshua ben Levi taught: "And whoever diligently studies the Torah repeatedly is exalted, as [Scripture] says: 'And from Mattanah to Naḥaliel, and from Naḥaliel to Bamot (Num. 21:19.'" From the formulation alone, it is difficult to determine the exact nature of the exaltation—whether mundane privilege merely, or (also or only) some form of spiritual transcendence. Nor will an analysis of the proof-text resolve the ambiguity, since the key term *bamot* is opaque in this context. Nevertheless, the use of these place names from the desert itinerary following the Song of the Well provides an instructive finale to these observations about the sages' understanding of Torah and its powers.

One may assume that Rabbi Joshua's attention was drawn to these toponyms in connection with Torah study for two reasons: first, because of the widespread exegetical association of Water and Torah; and second, because of the specific phrase which follows the Song: *umi-midbar mat-tanah* (v. 18). On the one hand, these words may be reasonably construed as an ecstatic conclusion to the Song (something like: "A gift [*mattanah*] from the desert [*midbar*]!"). At the same time, a contextual perspective supports the assumption that these words resume the desert itinerary interrupted by the Song (thus: the people travelled to Be'er [*be'erah*], from there to Midbar, from Midbar to Mattan [*mattanah; v. 18b*], from there to Naḥaliel, and on to Bamot [v. 19]). The occurance of this passage as a prooftext *in the context of the rewards of study*, suggests that R. Joshua combined both readings. As a rabbinic sage, his eye would readily perceive in the first phrase (*umi-midbar mattanah*), which precedes his proof-text, an allusion to the "Giving (*mattan*) of the Torah" in the desert (*midbar*) of Sinai. This being so, it would be natural to construe the toponymns in v. 19 midrashically. The result is the transformation of a spatial itinerary into a spiritual one: "And because of the Gift (*mattanah*) of the Law [the people of Israel] inherited God [i.e., they could say, literally, *naḥali'el*, 'God is my inheritance']; and because of this Inheritance they gained Heights (*bamot; literally, 'high places'*)."

The precise exaltation due to Torah study may remain ambiguous here, but one can hardly overlook the remarkable assertion which underlies the use of this biblical passage: that through Torah one inherits God. For the sages, as our context teaches, this divine inheritance is the grace of *the study and interpretation* of Torah. With this bold assertion, grounded in profound conviction, the development from scribalism to rabbinism is complete. No mere scribal custodians of the letters of Scripture, the sages know themselves to be the faithful students of divine truths—truths which may ever burst forth anew from their Source, like a well of living waters. The Beloved Companion may even hope to be a conduit of this stream. In such hope, the profound abyss between Revelation and Interpretation may be obscured—or transcended.

·III·

HERMENEUTICS, SCRIPTURE, AND THE PRESENT HOUR

·6·

THE BIBLICAL DIALOGUE
OF MARTIN BUBER

Characteristic of Martin Buber's literary and religious genius was the way he filtered traditional teachings through the depths of his soul. Much like Rilke, who once spoke of the range of raw living that was necessary "for the sake of a single line," Buber considered it a hermeneutical imperative to hear the words of ancient texts and transform them through the power of a personal and engaged receptivity. Or, to apply to this context a remark he made near the end of *I and Thou,* in connection with prophetic hearing: "to relate (*lauten*) means to translate (*umlauten*)."[1] An example of the correlation between true study and transformed living is expressed in the following vignette.

> Rabbi Eleazar said:
> When the Lord perceived the unjust deeds of the generation of the Flood and the generation of the Tower of Babel, He hid the Light of the first day of Creation from them.
> —For whom did He hide it?
> —For the righteous to come.
> —Where did He hide it?
> —In the Torah.
> —If so, what will the righteous who will find some of the hidden Light in the Torah do?
> —They will show it in their way of life.

Anyone familiar with the gnostic and eschatological character of this Hasidic teaching will marvel at Buber's ability to transform a mythic homily on salvific secrets into a dialogical instruction for the here and now.[2] So powerful, in fact, is this discourse that modern man may yet feel a portion of its truth enacted in his heart: a lost ray of creation that tints the dark void; a fleeting fragment of hope, reminiscent of Maimonides' account of the broken witness to revelation that unperfected mortals may

---

Portions of this chapter were first published in "Martin Buber As an Interpreter of the Bible," *Judaism* 27 (1978), 184–95, and are included here by permission.

experience in this world. But just what is this ancient Light? Or to pose the question more midrashically: To what may this "Light of creation"—still preserved in the secrets of Scripture—be compared? For Martin Buber, I think, the answer is clear. The world-building Light of origins may be compared to the world-building speech of God—for this speech, through the narrative voice of Genesis 1, brings an imaginable world into being; and through the ever-renewed voice of God in the Bible, calls mankind to authentic existence.

Let us speak more biblically. In the beginning, for Buber, was the word: not as some first creation or some hypostasized Logos, but rather after the manner in which the old Jewish Palestinian Targums render the opening words of Genesis: "with the word (viz., with speech) the world was created." Speech is thus a dynamic, divine reality, an ever-renewed power that lies at the source of creation. Indeed, for Martin Buber the divine speech which calls the world into real being initiates a "Dialogue between Heaven and Earth"—of which we are the latter-day respondents or speech partners. Correspondingly, as a collection of speech-acts the Bible is a great literary expression of this ongoing divine-human dialogue: a witness not only to its earthly triumphs, but to its all-too-human failures as well. To be open to the speech of the Bible is thus to be attentive to our inescapable participation in this dialogue—to its great responsibilities and demands. Accordingly, the urgency of *Bibel lesen* (or "Bible reading," as Buber's enterprise was often called) is nothing less than a world-renewing event. For to engage in authentic *Bibel lesen* is to pass from mere *lesen* to the *Geschprochenheit,* or "spokenness," of the text—and thence to the *Geschprochenheit* of our own life. And this is a new human beginning—in and by the word.

I

In an early essay imbued with the turn-of-the-century spirit of "Orientalism," Buber had the following to say about "the Jew of antiquity"—a human "type" which he hoped to renew amidst the mute ruins of modern (Occidental) civilization. "The Jew of antiquity," he said, "was more acoustically oriented (*Ohrenmensch*) than visually (*Augenmensch*), and more temporally oriented (*Zeitmensch*) than spatially (*Raummensch*). Of all his senses he relied most heavily upon his hearing when forming his picture of the universe."[3] For Buber, this *Ohrenmensch-Zeitmensch* has special value (as against his countertype, the *Augenmensch-Raummensch*); for he lives in the humanness of time—a time in which living unfolds periodically, and not through encompassing visions or generalizations. Time, moreover, is a modality for speech and hearing; for address and response. Thus the

Ohrenmensch-Zeitmensch—to continue this phenomenological characterization—listens and responds to the voice of the hour, responds and
changes with the tasks of time. No passive spectator, he is responsive and
attentive to the give and take of the moment.

Now this "Jew of antiquity," thought Buber, has left us a literary witness to his life of hearing the call of the hour—the Hebrew Bible (or
Miqra—which in rabbinical Hebrew means "calling out"). "Is it a book we
mean?"—asked Buber and Rosenzweig. "We mean a voice; and do we
believe our task is to read? We believe our task is to listen for the spoken
word. We want to reveal the word in the moment of its utterance."[4] The
task of Bible study is thus to penetrate the language of the Bible and to
attend to its "spokenness," its *Gesprochenheit:* for just here is the great
instruction of the text. Indeed in a later, powerful essay entitled "Biblical
Humanism," Buber returned to the earlier polarity of *Ohrenmensch-
Zeitmensch* vs. *Augenmensch-Raummensch*—though under different rubrics
and with a specific concern to articulate the peculiarity of the Bible as a
text. For him, this text is a document which embodies the living spirit of
encounter between God and persons in time—the meetings and the
responses. The words which the Bible contains thus enclose this mystery
of primacy. Indeed, insofar as this "great document . . . [is] grounded in
the ordering and directing word," it will regenerate "the normative primal forces" of the individual who attends, and so elicit a "concrete transformation of our total . . . lives"[5]—lives that can respond to the demands
and decisions of the moment. "Only that man who wills to do and hear
what the mouth of the Unconditioned commands him is a man worthy of
the Bible; only he "who lets himself be addressed by the voice that speaks
to him in the Hebrew Bible and who responds with his whole life."[6]

Surely one can hear in Buber's phrase "only that man *who wills to do and
hear* what the mouth of the Unconditioned commands him" a verbal
allusion to the response of the ancient Israelites to the Sinai revelation:
"we shall do and we shall hear" (Exod. 24:7). Buber thus wants all persons to place themselves before this great imperative: the imperative of a
life of dialogical response to the voice which speaks out of the moment.
And the document which may truly teach this renewal of personhood
and "response-ability" is the Bible—precisely because in the Bible words
reside "not in form but in originality (*Ursprünglichkeit*)," in the "immediacy of spokenness (*Gesprochenheit*)."[7] The words of the Bible are thus
words that create an event (*Geschehen*) of encounter in time. They are
concrete words for an *Ohrenmensch*, who lives concretely as a *Zeitmensch;*
not the stylized and formal works of Greek antiquity, the "detached
and . . . perfected" forms which delight the *Augenmensch*.[8] Thus the Bible
releases the primal forces of Sinai—of response and commitment—to
those who hear in it the voice of divine Instruction. "Untransfigured and

unsubdued," says Buber, "the biblical word preserves the dialogical character of living reality."[9]

Buber's task as a teacher of the Bible was thus to make the "immediacy of spokenness" of the Bible manifest, so that its primal powers might address the person and renew him as a *Bibelmensch:* for the tasks of life. For this reason his translations of the biblical text attempt to come as close as possible to the grain of raw spokenness. Indeed, these translations deliberately go against the grain of common chit-chat in order to awaken in the reader the mystery of speech and its transforming effects. Listen— and you will hear how the variability of Hebrew verb forms pulse through correlated German combinations to intone the mystery of speech. Listen more deeply—and you will sense the mysterious relations of living language: the relations between the concrete and the metaphorical, between the verbal and the nominal, and between the outer text of discourse and the deeper texture of verbal concourse.

The concreteness of Buber's translations shatter the "leprosy of fluency" of our habitual readings; and the emphasis on the root concreteness of Hebrew words even cuts against the assumptions of Western consciousness. Thus, for example, by the fact that one Hebrew word, *ruah*, is used in Numbers 11 to characterize both the 'spirit' of God's grace *and* the natural 'wind' brought by God, Buber hoped that the attentive reader would hear beyond the Greek dualities of spirit and nature, to the deep unity of the created world as inscribed in the Hebrew language. *Braus* and *Geistbraus* in the book of Numbers are thus the two pinions of the one wind-spirit that soars over the waters and gives mankind the breath of its deepest being.[10]

Beyond such matters, Buber's biblical work is further concerned to bring out the deeper verbal tones which unite the text at its profoundest levels of instruction. Thus Buber does not let the reader be satisfied with simple surface observations, but plunges him ever more deeply into the "suprapoetic" unity of a text—a unity which makes certain analytical distinctions arbitrary and, in the deepest human sense, uninstructive.[11] Study must be in the service of understanding the Bible "as the basic documentation of the Unconditional's effect on the spirit of the Jewish people"; it must be "an understanding that is service (*dienendes Wissen*)."[12] And so the reader is repeatedly urged and challenged to become a listener—an *Ohrenmensch*, who attends to the recurrence of the tones and phrases which evoke the deeper coherence of the text. In this way, the listener to texts may become a hearer who is sensitized to the oscillating rhythms of speech in all its human breath-units, disjointedness and hopefulness. Hearing that first and foremost "a psalm is outcry and not poem, [and] that a prophetic speech is not properly formal elocution,"[13] modern man will be instructed biblically. That is: he will not simply be informed with factual knowledge, but will be reformed by the deeper knowledge that the word which is given to one in life is no Logos which eternally is, or which may be possessed. That word is, rather, a word which "comes to be": for "the only being of a word resides in its being spoken."[14] Biblical language is thus no abstract formation (*Gebild*) but an event (*Geschehen*) of immediacy."[15]

II

The words of the Bible, as events of spokenness, thus instruct us in the dialogical character of reality. And the human and historical events reported in the Bible teach us correspondingly. As the great witness to the "Dialogue between Heaven and Earth," says Buber, the Bible records both the impact of the Unconditional upon the life of Israel *and* Israel's response. God demands the *whole* of life, and He wants man's unconditioned submission and response to Him in the totality of his life. "Thou shall be *whole (tamim)* with the Lord your God." This verse from the book of Deuteronomy (18:13) was heard by Buber as if to say: "You who are addressed and singled out as a 'Thou,' live authentically with your God through an unconditioned response to His words which (through the mouth of persons) create the world anew every day; and live without self-serving idolatries. For, '*Hear*, Israel! Our God is *One* Lord.' "[16]

The primary and fundamental expression of ancient Israel's drive toward unity under God is, for Buber, the Kingship of God. Israel first experienced God's leading presence at the time of the Exodus and, in covenantal joy, proclaimed Him as King in Jeshurun (at Sinai). The Sinai covenant thus symbolizes the reality of God's sovereignty over the entire life of Israel. But this covenant is no contract, no objective form. It is, rather, "an assumption into a life-relationship . . . comprehending the entire life of the men involved."[17] What God requires of Israel in the "Eagle Speech" of Exodus 19 is, according to Buber, the "unlimited recognition of the factual and contemporary kingship of God over the whole of national existence."[18]

On Buber's understanding, this theocracy of the covenant, this primal expression of Israel's life and faith, degenerated with the death of Joshua. In the end, theocracy was replaced by a king of flesh and blood. With the ascension of David, the dialogue with an all-ruling God, who claimed such leaders as Abraham and Moses, was fractured. Only the hope remained— the messianic hope embodied in Davidic imagery—of a true turning in unconditioned response to God alone. Indeed, for Buber, with this shift from a divine to a human kingship the deep dialectic of history set in. As poignantly expressed in the broken discourse of Scripture, the long course of external history is the history of failed, compromised and imperfect responses to God. Nevertheless, the true center of Israelite religion is the recurrent struggle—in and through the travail of time—to preserve the mystery and dominion of God beyond all "dogmatic encystments." Moses begins this struggle against all attempts to "have" or "utilize" God. His burden is shouldered by the prophets who follow. It is they, in the insistence and power of their lives, who repeatedly bear witness to the ideal of a divine kingship.

Withal, these true servants of God's unity suffer for God's true Kingdom. Repeatedly spurned and silenced, the community wants no part of the prophets' call and ignores God's ever-renewed address to "turn" away from idolatry. The people are deaf to the call of God's Kingdom: the challenging voice of the moment which, in the guise of the prophetic "other," addresses one to live in reciprocal freedom with God. For Buber, then, the true prophet is neither world-weary nor apocalyptic. As against the counsels of despair or the claims of foreknowledge, the prophetic word gives new direction and new freedom. Challenging the gnosis of intricate certainties (in all its cultural forms), the prophet stands firm in the abyss of history. He is the prototype of the dialogical man who, despite the despair and struggle of the moment, turns his whole being to God in freedom and responsibility.[19]

Martin Buber thus taught a teaching of God the Creator, who renews His world each day for the person who opens himself truly to Him. He taught that man must hold his ground in concrete life—against the temptations of secret knowledge or silence. If he does so, he lives in faith: in *emunah*. Thus for Buber the core of biblical faith is precisely this trustful turning to God who has been, and promised to be, a Present One. Indeed, says Buber, God who is the creator addresses man through His creation just here in lived concreteness, just when man knows himself to be addressed as "Thou"—and this is Revelation.

However, this notion of Revelation as address and response in the immediacy of life is not a revelation of law. For Buber, God becomes present as an addressing Presence that is neither general nor abstract. For this reason, and also because God reveals His Presence anew every moment, Buber rejected a once-and-for-all Revelation. Even at Sinai, when God was first proclaimed King in covenantal joy, there was no *general* Revelation. Even then, he argued, the One Presence was felt by all—by each and all, individually.

But there is more. This response to God in faithfulness at Sinai renews the pre-Sinaitic responses of Moses and the patriarchs—even as it renews the pledge of God to be a living Presence in the future as He was for past generations. For Buber, this renewed pledge is the core of the covenant. For though he acknowledged that the law is from Moses at Sinai, he strongly averred that the Sinaitic Revelation is *not* Law but entirely a revelation of Presence. Accordingly, when challenged that the Law is in fact an *absolutum* within Scripture, Buber could only respond that for him, as "a believing thinker, as a believing servant of the Truth," who hears the text in direct encounter and not as an "object of research," the Law is an accretion within Torah.[20] He acknowledged that many biblical laws do in fact bear witness to the kingship of God. But he maintained, nevertheless, that Torah is fundamentally instruction along the way of life—*not* a law above it.

However, if Torah is instruction along the way, and if it is renewed each moment through authentic human responses to the tasks of the hour, one may ask: Is God only "the God of a moment, a moment God?" Is spiritual continuity or Tradition possible? To these questions a positive answer does emerge from Buber's Bible interpretation—an answer which sees in each of these earthly moments of instruction a link in the chain of spiritual continuity. Thus, taught Buber, Moses understood the revelation to him at the Thorn Bush as a remanifestation (albeit in a new form) of the ancient God of the patriarchs. In this way, his immediate, momentary experience of God's Presence was deepened precisely as he recognized in it a deeper historical continuity. The chain of biblical leaders further discloses the abiding presentness of this God in the flesh of each historical moment. For they, too, recognize in God's revelatory Presence to them the remanifestation of the God of the covenant.

But what was a true conviction for Moses and the prophets was not equally true for their contemporaries. These latter did not so easily recognize in the promises and demands addressed to them the Voice of the ancient God of the patriarchs and the covenant. The turmoil of their historical lives, and the routinization of daily servitudes, hardened their hearts to any new response. Indeed, as Buber well knew, the servitudes of life and the fragmentariness (at best) of encounters with God have cut deeply into the heart of modern man as well. Buber therefore addressed himself repeatedly to the "eclipse" of God in our generation. One series of responses, pertinent here for their place among his Bible teachings, build upon the conviction that the *total* biblical corpus may serve as a paradoxical witness to God in our age of apparent divine absence.

Speaking to Jews in 1952 after the searing events of the Holocaust, and addressing himself to their sense of rupture with the historic God of Israel, Buber urged his co-religionists to be steadfast. He stressed that if they could persist in their memory of God's Presence as preserved in the Hebrew Bible, they could yet hope that, even after such deep darkness, they might again recognize their wrathful, loving God. The witness of the entire Bible would then, by its testimony to the past reality of dialogue between God and Israel, keep open the painful hope of renewed contact with Him.[21] In fact, already in the dark hour of 1941 Buber had spoken of the need to bear a patient suffering. Even in despair, he taught, dialogical man must say—for the sake of being whole with the God of all existence— "This [*too!*] is my God and I will glorify Him."[22]

Buber's remarkable transformation here of an ecstatic proclamation of divine Might (recited by the ancient Israelites upon liberation from historical bondage; Exod. 15:2) into a prayerful counsel for religious maturity in a time of despair, is a profound example of how biblical tradition may be converted into a living instruction. It manifests the tough yet tender demands to which dialogical man must submit himself: the narrow ridge of spiritual steadfastness which is dialogical living. Almost as a textual gloss on the preceding life-experiences, but now stated as an interpretation of the difficult passage in the book of Exodus (4:24–26) where Moses is attacked by the Lord during his return to Egypt, Buber explained the event as part of the inner-spiritual biography of Moses. After his commission, Moses had yet to be tested before the One who would be there as He would be there. Buber stated that the man of God has first to live through the reality that God is the source of All—the good and the evil. Only then can he be a true "sent one" (or prophet) in history. To be sure, one cannot know such a God cognitively. But one *can* be faithful to Him and His sovereign Unity by living steadfastly *through* the totality of experience as it presents itself. This teaching appears in his book *Moses*, published in 1945. It is strikingly anticipated by more meditative reflections on the subject in *I and Thou*, written a full generation (and another war) earlier.

III

In its profound concern with teaching the faithfulness to God required in authentic (dialogical) living, Buber's biblical work manifests a deep relationship between study and personal transformation. His way was truly a *dienendes Wissen*, an "understanding that is service." In a profound and subtle allusion to God's own Name, which he translated as the One who "is there" (*Ich bin da der Ich bin*), Buber stated that that person will hear the Bible's instruction who will correspondingly "be there" before the text[23]— attentive and listening. Study is thus in the service of life. It is a training for human listening. As we "read-hear" more profoundly, he believed, so shall we attend to the tasks of life more authentically. For as with life, all texts— and the text of the Bible most archetypically—resist "dogmatic encystments." The word of a text cannot be "had"; for there is no *Umfassung*, or encircling grasp of the living word. Rather, we enter a text as we enter dialogue—piecemeal; and we build up an interpretation dialectically—through corrections, queries and responses. This process, of course, is the famous hermeneutical circle; and its living dynamic, as we now see, is dialogical. In both cases (in living and in study), only readiness is a prerequisite: a readiness to hear and to be changed, to reject and to debate, to find oneself and to find another.

The Bible is thus a difficult book for modern man, says Buber. It is a book modern man "resists" just "because he cannot endure revelation"—that is, just because he cannot endure "this moment full of possible decisions" in which we must "respond to and be responsible for every moment."[24] Fleeing from such responsibility, modern man also flees from the Bible. And so, to draw one near to this text is to counsel the renewal of human speech and decision. There is no "mastery of the secret" here, but only "immediacy in facing it."[25] "The word is fulfilled, by way of individual man and the people, not in a perfected form (*Gebild*), but in proof of self (*Bewährung*)."[26]

> But this proof does not possess the permanance of the formed work; it exists only in the factual moment. Biblical humanism cannot, as does its Western counterpart, raise the individual above the problems of the moment; it seeks instead to train him to stand fast in them, to prove himself in them. This stormy, these shafts of lightening flashing down, this threat of destruction—do not escape from them into a world of logos, of perfected form! Stand fast, hear the word in the thunder, obey, respond! This terrifying world is the world of God. It lays claim upon you. Prove yourself in it as a man of God![27]

When Buber taught his texts, he taught them for the sake of holding firm in the terrors of time. He taught *Bibel lesen* for the sake of remaining a dialogical person—despite the will to power and flood of evil in our world. This was his teaching of the Psalms, especially. For the Psalms, he believed, give concrete expression to the human voice that struggles for *emunah*, or dialogical steadfastness in despairing times. Accordingly, whether one is a servant of the living word is proved through one's life—through *Bewährung*, as he says in the preceding citation (from 1933). But such proof of self, such a Bible-inspired steadfastness before evil, must be won anew each moment.

And so Buber taught this teaching repeatedly—but never so humanly as when he taught the Bible and the Psalms in Germany in the 1930s. In what has been recognized as a heroic act of spiritual resistance, Buber engaged in *Bibel lesen* and enacted dialogical steadfastness in the dark turmoil of history. Integrating the spiritual resources of a lifetime of biblical instruction, he manifested *emunah* through *Bewährung*. Many heard Buber's *Bibel lesen* and were renewed in their own commitment to the primacy and imperative of dialogue in our world. In our own times, when the cultural value of Scripture is not at all self-evident, Buber's biblical teachings may provide a similar renewal. Or at least this was his hermeneutical hope. Faced with an academic critique of his method and emphases—indeed, faced with an attempt to read Scripture as historical facts rather than living instruction—Buber might well answer after the manner of his response to Gershom Scholem's strong criticism of his Hasidic studies:

> Buber listened with great seriousness and with great tension. When I was done he was silent for a very long time. Then he said slowly and stressing every word, "If what you are now saying were right, my dear Scholem, then I would have worked on Hasidism for forty years absolutely in vain, because in that case, Hasidism does not *interest* me at all."[28]

·7·

MARTIN BUBER'S *MOSES*

"How small Sinai appears when Moses stands upon it," reflected Heinrich Heine in his "Confessions" of 1854. And he was not the only one to have this view. The towering figure of Moses has fascinated generations of creative writers from antiquity to contemporary times, and has inspired awesome portraits of this man of God and his life. An old rabbinical dictum has it that "each generation has its interpreters, each generation its sages." The point applies to the presentations of Moses, as well. Each generation has had its interpreters, and each generation has portrayed Moses in the light of its own image and concerns. Just think of the Stoic-philosophical *Life of Moses* by the great Jewish Alexandrian thinker, Philo (ca. 10 B.C.E.—45 C.E.); of the frescoes of Moses in the ancient synagogue of Dura-Europos; of the medieval Jewish "Chronicles of Moses, our Teacher" and the "Midrash on Moses' Death"; and, of course, of the mighty "horned Moses" of Michelangelo—itself the heir of an ancient artistic convention. In more recent decades Ahad Ha-am advanced his program of spiritual Zionism through an influential essay called "Moses" in 1904; and significant advances in modern Biblical scholarship were centered on studies devoted to Moses and his achievement (e.g., the essays of H. Gunkel in 1913 and 1930; and the books of H. Gressmann in 1913, and of P. Volz in 1907 and 1932). Arnold Schoenberg began his opera and text *Moses and Aaron* in 1932 (resumed in 1951), and Sigmund Freud published *Moses and Monotheism* in 1939. In September 1944, Martin Buber completed his own work called *Moses*. The book appeared in 1946, and a subsequent edition added the subtitle "The Revelation and the Covenant."

Buber's way to the Bible was not immediate. By the time of this new involvement, he was already famous throughout Europe as a translator and interpreter of world folk traditions (including his early renditions of Hasidic tales), and as a mystical thinker and proponent of spiritual Zionism. Reflecting upon these early years and his turn to the Bible, Buber

Originally published as an Introduction to *Moses* by Martin Buber (Atlantic Highlands, N.J.: Humanities Press, 1988), 4–12, and reprinted by permission.

published a poem in 1952 entitled *"Bekenntnis des Schriftseller"* ("Confessions of the Author").[1]

> Once with a light keel
> I shipped out to the land of legends
> Through the storm of deeds and play.
> With my gaze fixed on the goal
> And in my blood the beguiling poison—
> Then one descended to me
> Who seized me by the hair
> And spoke: Now render the Scriptures!
>
> From that hour on the galley
> Keeps my brain and hands on course,
> The rudder writes characters,
> My life disdains its honor
> And the soul forgets that it sang.
> All storms must stand and bow
> When cruelly compelling in the silence
> The speech of the spirit resounds.
>
> Hammer your deeds in the rock, world!
> The Word is wrought in the flood.

With these words, Martin Buber confessed the motivations and destiny of his literary work. These early years, he was to say, were a time of "readiness to make . . . testimony to the great reality of faith disclosed . . . through books and men." It was with the suddenness of a prophetic commission, in a manner reminiscent of the prophet Ezekiel, that Buber experienced himself as one seized by the hair and told, *"Nun stelle die Schrift!"* ("Now render the Scriptures"). From then on, he devoted himself to give "testimony to the great reality of faith" disclosed in *the* Book, and through its men of the spirit.

While Buber had grown up in the presence of the Hebrew Bible, he reported that early experiences with German translations had virtually closed the book to him. It was not until years later, in a moment of bereavement after Theodor Herzl's death, that he rediscovered the living word of Scripture. His plans in 1913, in the company of an interdenominational group of theologians, to translate the Bible free of traditional and stylistic encumbrances, were never realized. A new opportunity to achieve this goal arose at the overture of the publisher Lambert Schneider. Buber began to "render the Scriptures" in 1925, together with his great friend, Franz Rosenzweig. But Buber alone lived to finish the task in 1961, after many interruptions. The cultural achievement of his work was unparalleled; though in a speech delivered on the occasion of the completion of this labor of humanistic and spiritual scholarship, Gershom Scholem could not help but observe the irony that the German Jews for whom this work was done were no more, and the concern for a living speech that might empower its hearers was a chimera. Through the War and thereafter, speech and the image of the human had been trivialized—if not utterly desecrated.

The work called *Moses* was not the first of Buber's monographs or essays on the Bible. It was long preceded by a work on ancient Israelite messianism called *Kingship of God* (1932), by his joint essays with Rozenzweig called *Die Schrift und ihre Verdeutschung* (1935), and by his penetrating exploration of *The Prophetic Faith* (1944; the third part of the planned work on messianism). But as a work of his late maturity, *Moses* is a convenient place to review many of Buber's longstanding concerns with Scripture. For in this book Buber's methodological presuppositions about Biblical traditions and their recovery, his attitudes toward Biblical language and stylistics, and his views of the religious teachings of the Bible and their enduring value, all come to clear expression. Significantly, these three dimensions of Buber's biblical work have their structural parallels in the three basic areas to which ancient and modern hermeneutical studies have been devoted: (i) the theoretical concern with the methods and presuppositions of textual or cultural interpretation, (ii) the practical concern with the strategies of textual interpretation and historical reconstruction, and (iii) the cultural concern with the relevance or application of older texts to new life experiences and tasks.

But the true value of this correlation lies in the differences. For if Buber's tasks as a reader and interpreter of ancient texts were in part set by a long scholarly tradition of inquiry, he did not regard the foregoing three areas of hermeneutical study as separate domains. The isolation of theory from practice, and of so-called objective historical research from the enduring (subjective) teaching of a text, was not his way. These, he believed, were false and tendentious dichotomies. As against Western hermeneutics generally, Buber sought to integrate research, reading, and life instruction. This is a presupposition and recurrent expression of his life work that must constantly be borne in mind.

For Martin Buber, great texts like the Bible are genuine witnesses to the human and religious reality that precedes their literary formulation. This somewhat romantic conviction that the experiential kernel of a text is preserved in all successive renditions of it, and can be penetrated by the disciplined and attentive reader of later times, is a basic presupposition of his work. For this reason he was himself sharply critical, in his own "Preface" to *Moses*, of those scholars who approach the Bible as a series of literary strands far removed from the concrete reality of faith about which they speak; or who hope, at best, to reconstruct the literary kernels from which a narrative tradition has unfolded. These were and are the standard attitudes of the so-called Literary-Documentary and Tradition-History approaches to the biblical text.

Naturally, Buber did not deny that the reworkings of epic or any other traditions often tell us more about the generations transmitting the materials than about the kernels (literary or historical) which elicit these ongoing responses. But he felt that to let matters go at that is not only wrong-headed but unimaginative. For he felt, first, that other investigators were simply "dependent . . . on the theories of scholarly turns of thought," repeating their critical nostrums back and forth, without risking a more "unprejudiced critical investigation."[2] And he felt, further, that despite their "continuous process of crystalization," the ancient sagas preserve the original structures of experience, "which transformed the historical situation of the community."[3] The German romantic folklorist Jacob Grimm referred (in 1813) to such moments as ones of "*objektive Begeisterung*" ("objective enthusiasm");[4] and with his own master, Wilhelm Dilthey, Buber went on to believe that he could intuit and imaginatively identify with those primary experiences. To use Buber's own romantic terminology of other contexts, such an imaginative reliving of great moments of historical "enthusiasm" was a kind of literary *Erlebnis*—or dynamic, *enthusiastic experience through texts* of great moments of the human spirit. The result, Buber presumed, would be a true understanding of these moments, and a reciprocal renewal of the human reader who can attain to this level of imagination.

And so, in *Moses* Buber endeavored to penetrate behind the literary "crystalizations" of the Hebrew saga to the concrete historical experiences of Israel's religious origins. He believed himself aided in this effort through the very language of Scripture itself. Buber took the rabbinic word for Bible, *Miqra*, with all literal seriousness as a "calling out." By this he meant not so much a calling out or reading of the written Scripture, as the preserved outcry of the genuine "spokenness" (*Gesprochenheit*) of the events—as they were first articulated in the "spontaneously forming memory" of their human witnesses, and as they were continuously spoken forth by living tradition until the present literary witness had stabilized. The reader must therefore listen attentively to each speech-form, until the most primal one is intuitively heard, and one "hears" the Voice of the Divine Presence as it addressed the ancient Israelites in history. As an aid to that listening, the reader-hearer is advised to attend to the recurrent words and patterns of Scripture.

For Buber, the theme-words (*Leitwörter*) or key-words of the Bible are clues to the deepest meaning of the text—clues not solely to the apprehension of its literary sense and tradition, but to the underlying life experiences as well. This is a basic principle of all Buber's biblical work,

and it has profoundly influenced many modern readers. What Buber was
to say about the Psalms in 1952, shortly after writing *Moses,* articulated his
early and sustained presupposition anent biblical stylistics: "The recurrence of . . . key-words is a basic law of composition in the Psalms. The law
has poetic significance—rhythmical correspondence of sound values—as
well as a hermeneutical one: the Psalm provides its own interpretation, by
repetition of what is essential to its understanding."[5]

Significantly, the recurrence of theme- or key-words in the Biblical text
does not always conform to the regnant critical theories of how a given
text evolved from separate "documents." For that reason, the "reader of
the Bible" must "penetrate beyond this criticism to more profound distinctions and connections," as Buber said in his influential "Herut" speech
to Jewish students in Prague in 1918.[6] For again, literary "documents" are
not the starting point of biblical criticism for Buber—speech is, the
speech of experience preserved in theme-words and the "theme-word
style" that develops around them. In *Moses,* for example, the "thrice-
recurring 'he saw' and a rhythmically repeated 'his brethren' . . . indi-
cates . . . the more important elements" in the "narrative of the manner in
which Moses went forth to his brethren."[7] The biblical text thus calls out
its own interpretive scheme, urging the reader to attend to the unique
poetics of a particular unit. So attuned, the reader may then perceive
"profound connections" between this unit and other, more remote ones in
the biblical corpus. Anticipating modern literary theory, Buber thus developed his own appreciation of the Bible's profound strategies of intertextuality—whereby words in one textual unit allude to or transform
those found elsewhere. The result is that the Bible must be read as a
complex system of linguistic dynamics.

In all this, Buber's goal was neither an aesthetic nor an ahistorical
appreciation of the "literary structures" of the Bible for their own sake.
Rather, the purpose of such critical alertness to biblical language was to
properly penetrate the life of faith of ancient Israel, for the sake of an
historical understanding that is inseparable from a reader's self-renewal.
Buber thus had no use for programs of so-called objective, historical-
philological scholarship, which eclipsed the enduring meaning of the
text; nor was he interested in a private subjectivization of the text, which
obscured or ignored its concrete, historical otherness. For him, the two
approaches were one and inseparable—when properly pursued; and he
profoundly believed that his own hermeneutical presuppositions and
strategies of reading were conducive to that end.

But the relationship between "historical understanding" and "personal
transformation" is surely a delicate one; and with great men of the spirit,
like Martin Buber, the boundaries may often be completely obscured.
This is the case, I think, with Buber's *Moses.* For if the interpreter is correct

to find Sigmund Freud in the "Moses" of *Moses and Monotheism*, he will be no less correct to find Martin Buber and his thought in *Moses*. Perhaps the reason, in this case, has something to do with the intuitive method involved; for it can lend itself, unwittingly, to what might be called "hermeneutical transference," the projection of one's life agenda (and more) onto the text. Or perhaps we simply have here a case of largeness of spirit, of a massive intellect filling all the spaces of the text. Whatever the case, Buber believed that his dialogical thought as embodied in *I and Thou* was confirmed by the deep truths of the Bible; and that through study of the Bible (and Hasidism) his own thought was reciprocally nurtured and refined. Who can say? At best we may simply point to the remarkable affinity between the polar structures of "Egypt" and "Israel" in *Moses* and those which recur in all his other writings.

For Buber, Egypt and its pharaonic bureaucracy is, as it were, the embodiment of the "I-It" modality of human existence. This state is an impersonal civilization, oiled by routine and technique and manipulated by magic and divination. The goal is to control the gods, give form to the divine mystery, and legislate fixed patterns for all persons. This is far removed from Israel and Moses, so ideally portrayed in *Moses*, for this nation and its leader exemplify the "I-Thou" modality of human existence. Israel is directly "called" into being by God, and all as one assume the demand for "exclusive loyalty" which this delivering Presence addresses to them. The "assumption of a life relationship" which is not fixed, and requires Israel to live in freedom before the ever-new tasks of daily life, is the Covenant. No set of legal stipulations, the Covenant represents, for Buber, the assumption of a "living relationship" between God and People. It is the historical token of the readiness Israel expressed to respond to the Voice or Presence of God in history. Moses is the quintessential human expression of this willingness to accept the "rule of the Spirit" over his life, and to work for the unity of all life under God. The more weak-willed of the nation, by contrast, wish to "return to Egypt," which is the sin of trying to "have" God "at their disposal through the sacral system."

The tension between Moses and the rebellious people is thus, for Buber, the tension between those who would submit their entire life to God's kingdom, and those who would serve idols of their own making. Moses' rebuke of the people will be continued by later prophets, while the people's desire for a controllable God will be continued by their inevitable drive to fractionalize life into separate and manageable spheres—"politics," "religion," "ethics," and so on. Buber understood this biblical narrative as addressing a counter-imperative to mankind: to perceive the interconnectedness of life's tasks, and to work for personal and communal unifications under God. In *Moses,* and in Buber's thought generally, the faithful "Israel" of the Covenant serves the One true God of an "open-future"; whereas "Egypt" of the Pharaohs serves the idols who promise a "fixed-fate." This polarity was more fully exploited by Buber in an essay called "Prophecy, Apocalyptic, and the Historical Hour (1954)."[8]

And so, for Buber, a proper "historical understanding" of the Bible will lead to "personal transformation." Through the words of the text one is led to its authentic *Gesprochenheit* ("spokenness")—and this is to realize how the divine Presence addresses individuals in and through the events of life with the challenge of a total commitment to divine unity, to a concern for holiness and harmony in all actions. Attentive to this, the reader will not so much "have" new information, or be challenged by this or that particular commandment or episode. More profoundly, the lines of these various teachings will combine to change the reader in his or her relationship to existence and to other persons. And so, it is not so much that the Bible is an old text that must be applied to our contemporary condition. As a true text, which is to say, as a text that speaks truly of how God addresses His Presence to individuals in time, the Bible is an eternal text. Properly read, it is thus a text that may renew one's relationship to speech and to persons, and to the challenges of freedom for modern man.

In all this, Martin Buber speaks with a prophetic urgency. He wrote *Moses* in 1944, during a time of historical horror. "That Moses experiences [God]" as a living and challenging Presence, beyond form and information, "is what places [Moses] thus afresh in our own day, which possibly requires him more than any earlier day has ever done."[9] Certainly, one can read *Moses* as a response to the times: as a work that builds upon Buber's teachings to articulate, through the Bible, a statement on the true leader, on the true kingdom, and on the great uniqueness of Israel and its contribution to culture. Indeed, let us not forget a more demonic leader who ranted and killed in those times for the sake of another "kingdom," and against Jewish culture, which, he said, had given the world "the curse of Mount Sinai."[10]

But *Moses* is no mere moral homily against historical tyranny, with the Bible as its pretext or justification—in the manner of ancient rabbinic midrash. Or it is not only this. For *Moses* is, perhaps, also a more allusive midrash: one which, in the very process of historical inquiry, counsels a new understanding of God's presence in history, a more involved notion of scholarship, and a fully responsible awareness of the powers of speech. And this I say with all due respect. For as with all great midrash, Buber's exegesis of a biblical work transcends its subject, involving the reader in understandings and commitments that go beyond the text. To paraphrase an old rabbinic epigram: "The abstract midrashic reading of texts is not the main thing, but rather the transformation of these texts—through midrash—into sources of power for the renewal of personal and interpersonal life."

Whether Buber's method will rightfully yield accurate historical knowledge may not, then, be the true or final measure of his biblical *oeuvre*. The ultimate distinction of this work may rather lie in the particular *mode* of reading the Bible which Buber taught: a mode which unfailingly engages the reader at the very depths of his humanity, and challenges him to draw ever-new distinctions between "mere conscious being and true existence"—as Buber himself articulated his overall exegetical concern several years after writing *Moses*.[11] This suggestion that the enduring value of Buber's biblical teaching may lie more in its capacity to instruct moderns in self-understanding than in abstract historical knowledge is, perhaps, a paradox—precisely because the human instruction is received *in the very process of* historical inquiry. But if this is a paradox, it is so only in the manner of all midrashic paradoxes. For the truth of midrash is not the truth of historical information or textual analysis. It is the truth of the power of scriptural words to draw a reader into an authentic relationship with the mystery of the world—a world constituted by speech and the face-to-face relations which *Gesprochenheit* demands. To have taught us this, allusively, is Buber's enduring legacy. Beyond all dogmatism and fixed commandments, the Bible is for Martin Buber the rescued and ever-hearable speech of the living God. It is a Teaching which simply points out an ongoing way. This is also the teaching of midrash.

·8·

SPEECH AND SCRIPTURE: THE GRAMMATICAL THINKING AND THEOLOGY OF FRANZ ROSENZWEIG

In his characteristically forthright way, Franz Rosenzweig repeatedly addressed himself to the spiritual condition of modern man. One particularly powerful expression of this concern is found in his essay, "Scripture and Luther's Translation." "This man," he says, "is neither a believer nor an unbeliever."

> He believes and he doubts. And so he is nothing, but he is alive. Belief and unbelief "happen" to him and all that he is required to do is not run away from what is happening but make use of it once it has happened. This seems very simple when one has not entered the field of action, but it is actually so difficult that there is probably no one who has always accomplished it, [and] probably no one who has managed it on more than a very few, rare occasions.
> Whoever lives in this way can approach the Bible only with a readiness to believe or not believe, but not with a circumscribed belief that he finds confirmed in it. Yet even this readiness of his must be uncircumscribed and unlimited . . . [F]or such a man the days of his own life illumine the Scriptures, and in their quality of humanness allow him to recognize what is more than human, today at one point and tomorrow at another, nor can one day ever vouch for the next to provide a like experience . . . Not everything in the Scriptures belongs to him— neither today nor ever. But he knows that he belongs to everything in them, and it is only this readiness of his which, when it is directed toward the Scriptures, constitutes belief.[1]

Resonant with wisdom and challenge, this passage invokes a series of symmetries between living and reading. For both, authenticity demands the spiritual steadfastness to receive what is given in the here and now— without flight into the already known or the already written. Indeed, this combination of readiness (*Bereitschaft*) and resoluteness provides the only authentic presuppositions for modern man "who is nothing, but he is alive." It also produces a paradoxical moment rich in spiritual possibilities. For with the collapse of fideistic and philosophical presuppositions, modern man is thrown forward to new origins. Now everything may become hearable and sayable in unanticipated ways; now even the unraveled thread of ancient texts may be used to weave new textures of sense and purpose. The only precondition is the courage "not to run away from what is happening." But where can such courage come from, and what is the basis for the readiness to believe?

I

The blandishments of philosophy repeatedly tempt the timid spirit to exchange his fears of existence for the specter of pure thought. Upward from the concrete ground of life, the mind rushes to escape mortality through a Promethean attempt to reoriginate the self in ever more universal ideas of Mind and Self. The end of such bloodless abstractions is the utterly audacious claim "that death is—Nought (*Nichts*)."[2] But the cold fear of the earthly always returns man to his mortal origins and to the realization that cognition of the All cannot salve the "sting of death."[3] In fact, each and every death condemns this insidious deception of philosophy. The death-denying Transcendental Ego is thus negated by the cry of "Me! Me! Me!"—the voice of the mortal ego in time.

In this opening dialectic of *The Star of Redemption,* the merest word of self-affirmation ("Me!") revolutionizes the presumptions of philosophy.[4] It returns thinking to its existential base and thereby anticipates the triumph of speech over death itself. But only anticipates it; for however earth-bound and expressive, this 'Me' remains solitarily absorbed in its own mortality. In fateful desperation, this self-centered being imagines that it can conjure a world from itself; and so it does, repeatedly, in utter despair and disorientation. Inevitably, this spiraling self bores inward and proclaims its tragic isolation to be the very condition of mortal life. Only responsiveness to the claims of the hour can open the heart of this monologic self and give him the one thing needful—speech.[5] Thus the claims of existence pour down upon mortal man as the ever-present love of God. Acknowledging this love, the fettered self is inaugurated into a living dialogue with whatever "is happening." Language is therefore the authentic organon for understanding the life of man in time. And since biblical Scriptures witness to this truth, Rosenzweig uses its speech-acts as a vehicle for articulating the dialogical tenor of authentic life.

II

The silence and isolation of monologic man is broken by a double receptivity to the call of God. This call, in and through the forms of life, has been seeking man ever since he first construed his freedom as defiance.[6] Absorbed by his mortality, the adamic self remains blocked to God's repeated question: "Where are you?" It is only when this seeking voice calls him by his true name, "in a supreme definiteness that could not but be heard," that this solitary self ceases from hiding and responds "all ready, all soul: 'Here I am'" to the reality at hand.[7] Accordingly, this divine nomination is an evocation into authentic existence. For names are neither identical with things nor mere conventions (realism and nominalism are beside the point): they are rather speech-acts which create a seeable and sayable world. Thus when man hears himself truly named, he knows himself to be a creature and says "Here I am." Indeed, in this saying he becomes present to himself as an 'I' that corresponds to God's own Presence in the fulness of the world. For God's call is actually His eternal self-nomination: "I am the Lord (*Ewige*)'—that is, in Rosenzweig's language, "I am the Eternal." Hearing God's Name, then, man is himself named and responds with his own "I am present"—a condition of "pure readiness (*reine Bereitschaft*)."[8]

"Readiness" is thus an attitude, something like a structure of pure intention in time. In and of itself, it has no content; and it has only the vaguest of orientations until, without warning, it happens that a portion of the world is made manifest to the heart of man. This is God's command: "Love me!" As an imperative, "the 'Love me!' is wholly pure and unprepared-for present tense (*ganz reine, vorbereitungslose Gegenwart*)."[9] Such a moment, says Rosenzweig, is a miracle. It establishes a standpoint from which the indiscriminate plenitude of the world is reoriented—an axial moment from which the flow of happenings are co-ordinated as past and future.[10] And this radical reorientation of the self in space and time is nothing but—revelation.

As a pure imperative plus accusative, the "Love Me!" demands a response. And this it receives through the humble words: "I have sinned." This confession, whether voiced or unvoiced, is the deep grammatical structure of a movement of the self into relation. Before this, the 'I' was but a logical subject, turned in upon itself, desperately crying "Me! Me! Me!": I *plus* I *plus* I. Now addressed by the silent 'I' of God's speech (*I* love you), the implied 'you' of the addressee (*You!* Love Me!) becomes manifest as an 'I' as well. Each 'I' therefore becomes a 'you' for the other. From the human side, the side of reception and response, the infinite series of I *plus* I is replaced by I *and* Thou in correlation. Consequently, these conjunctions of 'and' establish living relations of reciprocity extending outward to redemption. From the side of God, each 'and' is a pure happening—a token of God's infinte love in which time is temporarily overcome. He who is "nothing but alive (*er lebt*)" and experiences (*erlebt*) this love (*Liebe*) knows the truth of the biblical word: "Love is as strong as death" (Songs 8:6).[11]

Here, then, is the core of Rosenzweig's religious anthropology. The human 'being' becomes an ensouled 'subject' as he responds to the summons of speech—God's eternal word ("Love Me!")—spoken anthropomorphically through the ever-changing face of existence.[12] As an imperative, this word is of the pure present: a manifestation of complete presence.[13] There is no *aporia* here precisely because this command is not a manifestation of a priori thought. The 'word' of God is rather direct and immediate,[14] and ever again inaugurates a hearer into time.[15] The fleeting, recurrent 'I' in the Song of Songs is the paradigmatic expression of this miraculous moment which, invariably, "sound[s] different but always mean[s] the same thing."[16] Corresponding to the affirmation of the 'other' implied by the imperative, the beloved soul affirms its own presence in love through the declaration: "for [truly] your love is better (*ki ṭovim*) than wine."[17] Negating all points of view in its comparative perspective, this affirmation becomes a grammatical "midpoint" in relation to which love's story (its narrative prelude) and love's hope (its precative prayer) may be spoken.

From its perspectival present, then, the beloved looks to its past. And since its re-origination in love feels like a renewal of the self and the world, it speaks of its own re-creation in the context of the creation of the world itself. Love's affirming "for your love is better (*ki ṭovim*)" thus "takes up the thread" of the triumphal "very good (*ki ṭov me'od*)" denoted in the narrative of creation, Genesis 1. As a paradigmatic structure, this adjectival celebration of the human as the pinnacle of creation reconfirms the more static predicate adjective "it is good (*ki ṭov*)" intoned in that text, as well as the even more silent 'Yea' expressed by 'Being' in the book of Nature.[18] Thus the logos of the elements, whose mute 'Yea' affirms the world as 'this' and not nothing, is now heard by the beloved soul as the intradivine speech of creation. Creation is therefore a religious revision of the logos of nature, re-lated by the affirming voice of revelation which comes to the beloved through the mouth of her lover. The voice of love in human communication is thus pre-dicted in the silent ground of reality. And just as love triumphs over death in the spokenness of the interhuman, so does the affirmative "it is very (*me'od*) good" phonemically predict this victory through the counterword: *mavet*, "death."[19] The consummate good of creation, its crowning affirmation, is thus the fact of mortality. Creatureliness is the truth of the world—and love is as strong as *mavet*.

But this prediction of victory is only in the ear of the beloved, who sees creation with the ever-present eye of love (and love's traditions).[20] It is not in creation as such, which is always past. This is so in experience, and so is it marked by the grammatical forms of Genesis 1. In this paradigmatic text, the preterit prevails: God *created;* the earth *was;* He *saw;* and it *was* morning. The creative imperatives of the present are "perfectly" recalled as past, completed action; and the variety of events are given syntactic coherence by the recurrent syndetic element 'and.'[21] This particle binds action to action and produces an epic narrative. This genre, Rosenzweig teaches, is always reflective of past occurrences—the shadow of the light of love which shines from the imperative born of the moment. In the profoundly reciprocal 'and' of true meeting, the 'and' of I *and* Thou, the light of the world is revealed; and this moment of affirmation establishes a point of orientation from which the world as a divinely affirmed fact is perceived in its syndetic unity.

Thus the conjunctive 'ands' of Genesis 1, which link the various days of creation, are the grammatical correlative of the human awareness that each thing "after its own kind" can emerge into the light of day—can be seen and affirmed in its own right. The light of the first day is therefore no unique event, and certainly no statement of the natural becoming of the elements. Rather, for Rosenzweig, this light is an attribute of the perceiving human consciousness which comes to know and affirm the elements as creations, as manifestations of God's ever-present love.[22] The attentive reader of Scriptures will therefore push beyond the narrative language of the text to theme-words like *ṭov* or arch-words like 'and' and hear as revelation what he also knows from his experience of love: that the hour of any day may reveal the light of God so that things are seen and affirmed for what they are.

The logos of love thus reveals the logic of the elements—the silent grammar of nature—as a divine creation. It also evokes a moment of dialogue: a logos-community of two. The mute other is now a speech partner—but only for the moment. God's eternal "Love Me!" is only partially parsed in each and every "love me!" said by one person to his neighbor. For so long as the divine Logos is broken by human logic, "[t]he world is not yet finished. Laughter and weeping are still in it. The tears are not yet 'wiped from every countenance.' "[23] The love of the nearest neighbor, which triumphs for the moment over death, is thus not yet an eternal triumph when all the world will be kissed by God's love. In the meantime, one must convert the (present) imperative "love me!" into the (future) precative "O, may you love me!" Indeed this duty to extend the power of love in the world was already predicted in the heart of love itself, in the beloved's bold desire to extend her love to all the world ("O that you were like a brother to me," Song of Sol. 8:1).[24] But love alone cannot grant this longing, since love is only in and of the moment. Accordingly, Rosenzweig teaches that this longing is only "fulfilled" in marriage and "the natural kinship community," and through "the bond(s) of a supernatural community." In a prophetic allusion to the kingdom of Heaven, Rosenzweig calls this sphere the *Reich der Brüderlichkeit*, "the realm of brotherliness."[25]

The language of community thus moves forward in hope from dialogue to communal song. The ecstatic affirmation of immediate love (*ki ṭovim*: "for your love is better than wine"), which retrospectively discloses the world as a divine affirmation (*ki ṭov*: "and God saw that it was good"), now exhortatively affirms this truth for all future moments (*ki ṭov*, sings the psalmist, "for He is good" [Ps. 136:1]). Divine monologue (the past indicative of creation) thus unfolds into the divine-human and interhuman dialogue (the present imperative of revelation); and these together give way, in hope, to communal praise (the precative future of redemption). But not quite; for this linguistic description of temporal development—from 'was' to 'is' and 'will be'—remains within the perspective of formal description. It does not reflect the grammar of experience, which is first 'you and I,' then 'it and he,' and only consummately 'he and we.'[26] This relation among the phrases is grounded in the truth of *Sprachdenken* (or speech-thinking), a thinking which moves from experience to thinking and not vice versa.[27]

In the choral chant of the community, the "individual I . . . estranged in all the distresses of a lonely heart" may yet "speak with the mouth of the congregation" and be transformed.[28] The intensification of the soul through identity with the neighborly community gives the solitary voice "the audacity" to sing: "Withal God is good (*akh ṭov*) to Israel" (Psalm 73:1).[29] Here is a supreme enlargement of the self through communal participation and hope. The recurrent celebration of this 'We' is proudly proclaimed in Psalm 115—a 'We' that is not "like them," who sink into the pit of speechlessness (v. 17) by their worship of dead idols, but a 'We' that embraces neighbors "like yourself" by virtue of their praise of the living God of love.[30] This community, in its realized and anticipated love, "drags all future eternity into the present Now" and knows that "'Not the dead'—indeed not, 'but we, we will praise God from this time forth and to eternity'" (vv. 17–18).[31] Death which is momentarily overcome in dialogue is now utterly defeated by communal prayer. Once again the words of Isa. 25:8 sound forth—now in an ever new formulation. "The We are eternal," he says; "death plunges into the Nought in the face of this triumphal shout of eternity. Life becomes immortal in redemption's eternal hymn of praise."[32]

The final (third) part of the *Star* builds upon these premises of community and celebration, and affirms the religious life of Judaism and Christianity. It thereby fulfills the governing languages of the two preceding parts: natural logos and dialogue. Thus whereas the organon of mute mathematics (in part one) precedes and predicts the organon of human speech (in part two), whose highest form is communal praise, the latter is succeeded by the organon of the sacred calendar and its grammar of liturgy and gesture.[33] On another level, we may say that this triadic structure of the *Star* translates into three successive books: the book of Nature, the book of Scriptures, and the book of Tradition; and that each of these texts is explicated by a distinct interpretative strategy: the methods of science, of speech-thinking, and of sacred commentary. Accordingly, the central concern of part three of the *Star* is to provide a reinterpretation of traditional worship. For Judaism, the community in which Franz Rosenzweig built his home, generational continuity through family life and communal piety is its "Fire" and "Eternal Life." Indeed just this perpetuity of praxis and progeneration is Judaism's share in the truth of God's love, the veritable seal of God Himself. No abstraction, this truth is in fact personified in the ever-present mouth and face of the beloved: in a kiss and the immediacy of the speechless gaze. As it is written in Scriptures, "Let him kiss me with the kisses of his mouth, for your love is better than wine." And it also says, "Set me as a seal upon your heart . . . for love is as strong as death . . . [and] her flames . . . a divine fire."[34]

III

Let us reflect more deeply upon this "as it is written"—a phrase used in rabbinical midrash to introduce a prooftext from biblical Scriptures, and one which has pivotal significance in Rosenzweig's thought. He refers to it just prior to his analysis of the Song of Songs, just after his meditations on love and aesthetics. He says:

> Under the love of God, the mute self came of age as eloquent soul. This occurrence we had recognized as revelation. If language is more than analogy, if it is truly analogue—and therefore more than analogue— then that which we hear as a living word in our I and which resounds toward us out of our Thou must also be "as it is written" in that great historical testament of revelation whose essentiality we recognized precisely from the presentness of our experience. Once more we seek the word of man in the word of God.[35]

This passage recalls our opening citation by virtue of the conjunction it evokes between life and texts; and by virtue of the assertion that Scriptures are a human witness to what is "more than human." Indeed, a close grammatical analysis of Scriptures is hermeneutically apposite to an understanding of life precisely because of the fundamental grammaticality of our human existence. Our own experience therefore confirms the "essentiality" of what "is written" in Scriptures, so that in seeking "the word of man in the word of God" we may encounter something of the divine speech to which human life is response and expression. This is no mere rhetorical ploy. Rosenzweig is insistent "that the distinction between immanence and transcendence disappears in language."[36] And so the "as it is written" is the "voice of God in human inscription"; and the hermeneutics of reading must therefore serve to recall man to the word of God that summons him into existence. One may therefore say that the horizon of textuality is just this divine-human speech resounding within the text. It is to these resonances that the reader must respond—but only insofar as he is also a hearer.

For this is Rosenzweig's hermeneutical circle. One becomes a hearer of Scriptures only by reading, but one truly reads this text only by hearing its graphic sounds. What is to be done? How is one rescued from the despair echoed by Rabbi Eleazar ben Azzariah's ancient query: "How then might I interpret Scripture in such circumstances?"[37] The answer lies in the nature of Scripture itself. For biblical Scriptures is no mere book, but the written traces of speech. For this reason it is not a *Schrift* for the eyes but a *Miqra* (Reading) for the ears. In re-citing its words, the reader arouses the in-scription from its monologic silence so that the voice of the text becomes his own call for dialogue with the eternal partner.[38] Deep calls to deep: a moment of presence happens, and time is defeated in a revelatory 'Now.' Accordingly, the possibility of interpretation arises in and through the speech-act of reading precisely because this reading may evoke a grammaticality correlated with the reader's own experiences. As with life, the only precondition here is readiness. On the other hand, the summons which addresses a person through Scripture is not "Love Me!" but— "Hear it from this!" *Shema' miney.*[39]

Since Scripture does not arise in an aesthetic act,[40] but through an event of speech, its "literary" forms always serve dialogical ends. For example, the genre of narrative may serve to actualize a "present" dialogue with the epic past,[41] just as the genres of instruction or prophecy may reorient one to the demands and potential of temporality. Each literary form (or *Gattung*) thus has its own *Sitz im Leben* (life-setting) which may be engaged through reading. There is no pregiven formula for this, though the very grammaticality of the text points the way.[42] Along the syntagmatic axis such pointers may include the way verbal tenses and nouns hang together in rhetorical sequences, as well as how such words may be intervocalically related (in one or adjacent textual units). Thus the repeated and diverse imperatives of the lover (the 'I') in the Song of Songs point to the fleeting and ever-new presentness of revelation, of its momentary "fulness" but ultimate partiality. As regards the redundancy of the same word in one text, its patterns of deployment may silently point toward a meaning. For example, the recurrent themeword *lo'* (no/not) in Psalm 115 serves to dramatize a variety of contrasts—in a way quite proper to the polemical tone of the praise; whereas the repeated themeword *tov* (good) in Psalm 73 marks the outer borders of the prayer and, by virtue of a strategic variation, serves to point out the spiritual development of the speaker (who moves from the generalization in v. 1 to the personal witness of v. 28). In other instances, themewords may also serve to coordinate diverse episodes along a narrative plane (like the moral nexus established between Genesis 27 and 29 via the verbal stem *rimmah* [cheat]).[43]

Along a paradigmatic axis, themewords which function intratextually can be perceived to realign intertextually—that is, along the coordinates of creation-revelation-redemption. The relations between the references to death in Gen. 1:31 (*ki tov me'od/mavet,* "for death is good"), Song of Sol. 8:6 (*ki 'azah ka-mavet ahabah,* "for love is as strong as death") and Ps. 115:17 (*lo' ha-metim yehallelu-yah,* "for the dead will not praise the Lord"), or between statements of affirmation in Genesis 1 (*ki tov,* "that it was good"), Song of Sol. 1:2 (*ki tovim dodekha,* "for your love is better") and Ps. 136:1 (*ki tov,* "for He [the Lord] is good") are two of many cases in point. They are used explicitly and strategically to this end in the *Star.* But in other instances, explicit comments on one word may evoke patterns otherwise quite latent. For example, Rosenzweig's remark that the "Spirit of God" in Genesis 1 is a wholly impersonal power (in creation) triggers associations with the personal use of this phrase in the context of revelation (cf. Gen. 41:38), and subsequently with a prophecy of its communal extension in messianic times (Joel 3:1–2).

Rosenzweig thus teaches the modern reader to perceive unexpected unities in Scripture via the temporal configuration of the "Star of Redemption." However, it must be emphasized that such paradigmatic readings are only hermeneutically compelling by virtue of the fact that they exemplify on a scriptural plane the unity which the temporal coordinates past-present-future have in ordinary life. For this reason, the intertextual patterns of creation-revelation-redemption are essentially prooftexts of life-patterns. Put differently, life is not so much an enactment of scriptural truths as Scripture is an inscription of human experiences. The classical relationship between text and commentary is thus reversed. Indeed, in Rosenzweig's understanding, the phrase "as it is written" actually introduces a commentary on life—since study of Scripture is a fundamental means of seeking "the word of man in the word of God." Starting from experience, Rosenzweig begins with the oral word, so to speak. The written Torah is the chariot of this holy spirit,[44] and ever again awaits the new voice of man to re-call it to its dialogical origins.

IV

What, then, is the validity of scriptural interpretation? What and where is its verification? For Rosenzweig, the answer lies in just that transvaluation of values that marks his New Thinking: in the "oral Torah" of living experience. Accordingly, to engage in abstract speculations about Scripture and predetermine what is either "believable" or "essential" is to produce empty "platitudes."[45] The validity of an interpretation only arises in and through the experience of study when, for each person in individual and ever changing ways, the inchoate teaching of the text (its *Lehrstoff*) becomes true Instruction (or *Lehre*).[46] Thus it happens that

> the days of [a man's] own life illumine the Scriptures, and in their quality of humanness permit him to recognize what is more than human. . . . This humanness may anywhere become so translucid under the beam of a day of one's life, that it stands suddenly written in his innermost heart; and the divine in human inscription becomes as clear and actual to him for that one pulse beat as if—at that instant—he heard a voice calling (*wie eine Stimme . . . rufend*) to his heart.[47]

The rhetorical power of this passage is carried both by the bold voice of the speaker and by its allusion to an ancient prophecy (Jer. 31:32). Indeed, Rosenzweig's reference to Jeremiah's eschatological promise of a new Torah to be divinely inscribed upon the hearts of the renewed people underscores his sense that, for modern man, a new covenant with God's word must be experienced as something like a personal revelation. The ontological truth of Scripture is thus only verified ontically—verse by verse, teaching by teaching—and only insofar as it becomes a subjectively experienced word. This is not to say that, as a historical *objectivum*, the "old covenant" was unimportant for Rosenzweig. Rather, I mean to emphasize that he was deeply aware of the hermeneutical chasm separating the old Scripture from its reinscription in the heart of modern man—and the need to mediate between these two poles. "Not everything (*alles*) in the Scriptures belongs to [modern man]," he observed, "neither today nor ever. But he knows that he belongs to everything in them." This trenchant formulation strategically reworks Ben Bag Bag's traditional dictum about Scripture and its interpretation: "Turn it again and again for *everything is in it*" (M. Avot V.22). In a manner characteristic of the New Thinking, Rosenzweig revises this teaching so that its a priori claim that "everything is in" Scripture is conditioned by the experiential priority of personal commitment to "everything in it."[48] Indeed, this experiential dimension is deeply marked by the very verb chosen to refer to one's belonging to Scripture: *gehört*. For through it we hear an echo of the fact that mere study becomes *Lehre*, authentic learning, when the voice of Scripture is "heard" in one's innermost heart. One must be always inclined to hear, Rosenzweig teaches; but one cannot always do so.

Perhaps you will hear here another hermeneutical circle. If so, note how Rosenzweig resolves it through his remark that "one hears differently when one hears in the doing"[49]—that is, that all one's presuppositions about what is believable and doable change through the actual experience of them. Once again, a traditional dictum has been revised— this time the well-known affirmation "we shall do and we shall hear" from Exod. 24:7. Earlier generations pondered the logical inversion in this ancient commitment to the revelation at Sinai—a commitment to doing before a commitment to hearing—and offered numerous interpretations. Rosenzweig retains something of the ancient tendency to read the two clauses of the verse consequentially ("we shall do *so that* we shall hear"), but he also collapses the parts into one dynamic exchange ("we shall hear *in* the doing"). He thus emphasizes both the personal and the experiential nature of authentic readings of Scripture. There is no pregiven proof or guarantee that this will take place—until it does; and therefore there can be no other "proof" of the decision to be committed to the centrality of Scripture in one's own life save for those moments wherein the text becomes "inner power"—a personal and lived truth. Here and here alone is the validity of scriptural interpretation—and its verification.

All this suggests that for Rosenzweig hermeneutics is part of a messianic theory of knowledge.[50] The textuality that confronts the reader as mere *Lehrstoff* is converted into *Lehre* word by word—as it is confirmed as a voice written in the heart. Accordingly, the eschatological moment to which Jeremiah refers means, for Rosenzweig, the interiorization of the text and its transformation into a personal expression—the renewal of "everything in it" through the life of each and every person. Thus, just as the primordial *Urstoff* of the world is transformed into the forms of creation through the discriminating power of light, the *Lehrstoff* of Scripture is transformed into direct instruction by the illuminating strands of one's life experience (what Rosenzweig refers to as the "*Lichtstrahl eines Lebenstag*"). Creation is therefore renewed and brought to light through each authentic reading of Scripture. Along a linear plane, the accumulation of these moments approximates, proleptically, an eschatological "All Day" of light—when all God's creation will be seen directly for what it is. However, each "day" of illumination already defeats time and anticipates eternity; for each hermeneutical renewal of creation derives from the "pure present" of a personal revelation which draws the future into its timeless 'Now.' Thus in the sacred moment when a portion of Scripture is heard as a voice calling to one's deepest self, the tenses of lived temporality converge into the *nunc stans* of eternity.[51] One may therefore only know a text word by word; but in the depths of each word there is the proof and promise of eternal life.

For Rosenzweig, then, the temporal path from history to redemption leads through the transformation of (scriptural) texts into empowered persons: one word at a time. At the same time, the validity of the hermeneutical act is verified only by life itself: one moment at a time.[52] You will recall how, at the beginning of the *Star*, mortal man resisted the sweet-talk—or should I not say, sweet-thought?!—of philosophy through a desire to affirm his existence in the rough and tumble of life: "*er will bleiben, er will—leben;*" "he wants to remain," says Rosenzweig, "he wants—to live."[53] And indeed, we have heard the extent to which Rosenzweig's whole instruction is to guide modern man to an affirmation of life—both through his mathematical meditations on the arch-word *Ja* (Yea) in Nature, and through his grammatical analyses of the theme-word *ṭov* (it is good) in Scripture. Accordingly, it comes as no surprise that both notes resound at the end of the *Star*. Discussing the fact that humans are truly creatures only by virtue of the fact that they cannot "see the whole truth," but must "remain within the boundaries of mortality," we now hear the confident affirmation of this fact in the words: "*Und wir wollen ja bleiben. Wir wollen ja leben* (And remain we would. We want to live)."[54] The addition of the particle *ja* (yea, truly) into this comment serves to underscore and confirm the teaching that mortal man lives his true creatureliness in the "portion" of truth which God "imparts" to him daily. To live fully is thus to overcome death momentarily: to live eternity in time.

> We cling to our creatureliness. We do not gladly relinquish it. And our creatureliness is determined by the fact that we only take part, only are part. Life had celebrated the ultimate triumph over death in the Truly with which it verifies the personally vouchsafed truth imparted to it as its portion in eternal truth. . . . In this Truly, it is creature.[55]

This profound affirmation of creatureliness in which death is truly overcome also recalls the opening pages of the *Star*, and sounds the death-knell of philosophy for all but the last time. The final chime is muted within Rosenzweig's discussion of the scriptural words written over the gates of life, the words of the prophet Micah: "He has told you, o man, what is good (*mah ṭov*), and what does the Lord your God require of you but to do justice and to love mercy and to walk humbly with your God."[56] For Rosenzweig, the true life-affirmation, the great *ṭov*, is "to walk humbly *with* your God": to be "free of every condition" and so live "wholly" in the "Today" of eternal truth. As against the presuppositions of philosophy, such living "dares at every moment to say Truly to the truth (*zur Wahrheit Wahrlich zu sagen*)."[57] Here, once more, is the deep dialogical ground of existence reaffirmed: to walk *with* God is to *say* Truly to God's truth, to respond with unconditional trust to His ever-present word in life.

And just what is this Truly (*Wahrlich*)? Rosenzweig calls it the "*gesprochne Ja und Amen* (the spoken Yea and Amen)."[58] This correspondence of terms deepens the hermeneutical dimension of the affirmation of creatureliness cited above: "Life had celebrated the ultimate triumph over death in the truly (*Wahrlich*) with which it verifies (*bewährt*) the personally vouchsafed Truth (*Wahrheit*) imparted to it as its portion in eternal truth." As the very language of the passage declares, truth is lived and verified in the course of life. But now that we know that *Wahrlich* is also Amen, can we not also hear in these words Rosenzweig's profoundly serious midrash? For the life-affirming word Amen (Truly) is the base for the biblical words *emet* (truth), *emunah* (faith) and *ye' amen* (verify). Accordingly, the biblical "translation" (so to speak) of the passage would have it that in the response of "Amen" to life one faithfully affirms its truth. Faith is thus the affirmation of the truth with one's whole life; and the word Amen is a life-act so wholly of "Today" that it partakes of eternity.

This hermeneutical conjunction of "faith" (*emunah*) as a life-act and "truly" (*amen*) as a speech-act has its ancient echo in a remarkable midrashic teaching taught by the sage Resh Lakish (*b. Sanhedrin* 119b). He said: "Whoever answers 'Amen' with all his strength, for him the gates of paradise are opened. As it is said [in Scripture, Isa. 26:2]: 'Open ye the gates that the righteous nation, who preserves faithfulness (*shomer emunim*), may enter.' [Thus, said the sage:] Do not recite [Scripture as it is written] *shomer emunim* (who preserves faithfulness) but rather *she-'omerim amen* (who say Amen)." For modern man, doubtful about transcendence, this oral Torah has a disturbing voice. For it teaches that the human word of affirmation is a response—in life and through life—to the Word which calls. Spoken with strength, this "Amen" opens the gates of paradise—and this is transcendence in time.[59] Thus spoke Resh Lakish; and thus does he prophesy Franz Rosenzweig's *Lehre* of life as liturgy.

·9·

THE TEACHER AND THE
HERMENEUTICAL TASK:
A REINTERPRETATION
OF MEDIEVAL EXEGESIS

There is a question that arises again and again as I walk into class or do research. It is a question that probes the tasks and responsibilities of the teacher-scholar in the community. That question is: What does it mean to interpret and teach texts? What is involved in their presentation and transmission, and how, in fact, does one learn from them? These issues are sharpened by the realization that while the questions are asked in the present, that which is taught and interpreted relates to both past and future. The present—in which teaching, interpretation and transmission converge—is the pivot between memory and hope.

Something of this paradoxical and problematic situation is indicated by Plato, in the last part of the *Phaedrus*. There, through the observations of Socrates, a dilemma appears.

> . . . anyone who leaves behind him a written manual, and likewise anyone who takes it over from him, on the supposition that such writing will prove something reliable and permanent, must be exceedingly simple-minded . . . if he imagines that written words can do anything more than remind one who knows that which the writing is concerned with.[1]

But what about us late-comers? What can these words remind us of if we do not *already* know "that which the writing is concerned with?" Is there any hope to understand the traces of a text unless it is part of our experience? And if this experience is precluded just because we are late-comers, is there a cultural condition which nevertheless retains some link

A version of this essay was originally published in the *Journal of the American Academy of Religion* 43 (1975), and is used here by permission.

to the "concern" of the text? Given this problematic, the solution of the ancient rabbis is most impressive. For they claimed that all their teachings originate (at least in principle) at Sinai—coterminous with the revelation of Scripture itself. As a result, an unbroken chain of tradition—from the first hearing of the words to the present historical hour—guarantees the possibility of legitimate interpretation.[2] "Moses received the Torah at Sinai and transmitted it to Joshua, and Joshua to the Elder, and the Elders to the Prophets, and the Prophets to the Men of the Great Assembly" (*M. Avot* I.1).[3] Arab tradition also understood the fundamental significance of *'isnad*, a chain of tradition.

Plato's inquiry, and so our own, is expanded by another remark.

> You know, Phaedrus, that's the strange thing about writing, which makes it truly analogous to painting. The painter's products stand before us as though they were alive, but if you question them, they maintain a most majestic silence. It is the same with written words; they seem to talk to you as though they were intelligent, but if you ask them anything about what they say, from a desire to be instructed, they go on telling you just the same thing forever.[4]

The text maintains a "majestic silence." It neither acknowledges nor responds to the many new, interpreting words which address it. After the text has ceased to speak, all that is heard is the voice of the interpreter. But these words of the interpreter have a dialectical function as well: for despite their alien distance, they dare cross over the historical gap and mediate whatever latter-day communication a text might yield. As mentioned, the ancient rabbis believed that their oral teachings could release the written words of Scripture for each generation (cf. *Tanḥuma, Noah*, 2).[5] Revelation occurred once, written and inscribed; but human learning, they believed, is perpetual, oral and described. Nevertheless, it is precisely the many interpretive words of the rabbis that attest to their ultimate distance from Sinai, and to the majestic silence which the written words maintain before and after all exegesis.

Such, then, are some of the problems of alien and silent texts as they impinge upon the teacher and scholar. In what follows, I would like to reconsider the question of interpreting, teaching and transmitting texts through a reinterpretation of a traditional mode of exegesis.[6] In the Middle Ages, Jews and Christians elaborated a fourfold method of scriptural interpretation. Jews called it *PaRDeS*—an acronym for *Peshat*, the literal meaning; *Remez*, the allegorical meaning; *Derash*, the tropological and moral meanings; and *Sod*, the mystical meaning.[7] The eternal nature of Scripture reveals itself here as a well of living waters, releasing different and simultaneous dimensions of its words to all hearers at all times.

Admittedly, a differentiation of strategies for reading and levels of meaning could be formulated more neutrally than through medieval categories. But my concern in presenting a hermeneutical organon as a midrash of *PaRDeS* is not to claim that this schema is the only or best analytical systematization of interpretation. My concern is rather to re-frame modern text study through the schemata of sacred learning—wherein each level of interpretation requires a different orientation to the text and discloses different dimensions of truth. The integrity of the text is thus the fulness of all these possibilities, even as it is the integrity of the reader to meditate this fulfillment. In *PaRDeS*, textual sense and human sensibility are dynamically interrelated.

In the ensuing discussion, I shall use biblical scriptures as my textual material. But it should be obvious that what I say of this Scripture is paradigmatic for text study generally—and perhaps for a broader cultural hermeneutic as well.

I

Peshat is the literal sphere of text interpretation. But what is a "literal" meaning, and what does a "literal understanding" of a text mean? The matter resists facile definitions. We might say, for starters, that the literal meaning is the text at its face value—the text taken in terms of the conventional meanings of the words. But does this not reduce the literal meaning to either a socially relative or perhaps banal sense?[8] And even if this definition often helps, it is not comprehensive. What is the literal meaning of a metaphor or a simile? Certainly their significations are independent of literal, lexical sense, and depend upon an established cultural code (consider such expressions as Richard the Lion-Hearted; foot of a mountain; smart as the devil). Moreover, we are also well aware that many words are polysemous or ambiguous, that their lexical range is broad and dense. Certainly such factors create difficulties for any simple definition of the "literal" meaning.

There are other considerations. Let us take, for example, the opening phrase of the Hebrew Bible: "In the beginning of God's creation of heaven and earth" (Gen. 1:1). Are we to understand this literally, as a witnessed report, or as a theological construction? If the latter (and it is the result of reflection and tendentiousness), how do we assess its literalness in relation to the "fact" of creation, or to the numerous variant traditions preserved in Scripture (cf. Gen. 2:4b-25; Pss. 74:13–17; 89:9–11)? And if the symmetrical design of Gen. 1–2:4a is its dominant feature, what is the literal meaning of this text in relation to itself—especially given the logical difficulties (between days one and four, or two and five) which have bothered readers since antiquity?

We may press further with related reflections on Gen. 32:25–33, the well-known text regarding Jacob's night strife with a divine being at the Jabbok ford. Is this the report of an actual strife, or does it reflect Jacob's inner struggle with himself? Is it perhaps a dream or even an allegory of the nation—insofar as Jacob is named Israel? Surely such a reading is not out of the question, given the inner-biblical midrashic variations of this episode in Hosea 12. And how would an ancient Israelite have understood it? It would certainly be limiting to suggest that the "literal" purpose of this text is merely to provide an aetiology for the northern shrine of Penuel, or for the custom of abstaining from the sciatic nerve of animals. It is also apparent that even if we understand the separate facts of this or another text, its total, "literal" meaning is even more complex.

Given these considerations, among others, it would appear that a revaluation of *Peshat* is necessary if it is to serve any systematic (or at least stable) function in the interpretation of texts. But where can we begin? What constitutes the ground-level literalism of a text? I would suggest that it is both the discrete words of the text (its graphic units of construction) and the factual phenomenon of the whole. Each word is literally itself, and no more; the text is only itself, and that is all we have. This is not the level of value, but the ground-level of facticity. At this basal level of literalism, a text is the ever redundant presentation of itself—its own 'thisness.' This textual level is dramatized in Sephardic Jewish liturgy. Prior to the public reading of the Torah on the Sabbath, the congregation points to the scroll and declares: "*This* is the Torah which Moses set before the Israelites—according to the word of God by the agency of Moses." To be sure, it is the 'thisness' of the Torah which is given *to* reading. But such an inscribed text is no more a level of interpretation than the fact of a book or a page which is given to be read. As a received datum, this 'thisness' is what Santayana called "concretion in existence."

The *Peshat* thus focuses on the givenness and autonomy of the text, on its independence from the words of interpretation. The words of the text are all that we have. And so the first task of teaching and interpretation is to take the textual artifact seriously. This means recognizing the essentially dualistic relationship the interpreter has with the text. Its words are not his words, nor its thoughts his own—at least not initially. A text-dialogue must acknowledge the independent integrity of both text and interpreter. The text must be allowed to open the relationship without any preconceived tendentiousness. We recall the words of Rabbi Ishmael, who chided Rabbi Akiva: "Indeed, you say to the text, 'Be silent until I interpret'" (literally, 'until I give a midrashic interpretation').[9] That is, he accused the sage of not letting the text present itself.

Insofar as the literal nature of a text consists of its units of construction, one may be struck by a variety of observable phenomena—be these the length of sentences or their design on a page. We may note, for example, that the Massoretic tradition presents the poem in Exodus 15 linearly (called "brickwork"), while that in Deuteronomy 32 is arranged in parallel columns. But such arrangements are no more interpretations of the text than is Handel's optical device when, in a chorus on Exodus 15 (relating how the waters "stood like a wall"), he printed the notes in vertical rows![10] Accordingly, in our revaluation of *Peshat* all interpretative construction is preceded by the destruction or suspension of all preconception before the textual given. The teacher must lead the student through such a dialectical process. Moreover, recognition of the human construction of meaning leads (by another dialectical turn) to the insight that the text itself is a constructed form. An analysis of the modes of such construction is the task of the two succeeding levels of *PaRDeS*.

II

Remez is the allegorical sphere of text interpretation. It is here that the dialogue between text and interpreter produces meanings. This dynamic between a text and an external code which explains it, or translates it into another context of meaning, is the central phenomenon of allegory upon which my reinterpretation is based. Accordingly, we may say that the *Remez* involves the determination of significance by means of factors independent of, and external to, the textual surface (the *Peshat*).[11] Thus to the extent that texts represent personal or historical experiences, or posit certain phenomenal realities, these representations and propositions are interpreted by means of something (facts, words, or ideas) *outside* it. Such correlations (be they ever so latent or prereflective) help constitute the meaning at hand.

The extent to which there is agreement between the *Peshat* and what it "means" depends upon methodological conventions and periodic preferences. This process begins with the lexical code. For if we understand "silly babe" or "jealous God" in terms of twentieth-century discourse, and not in terms of elizabethan usage, we do not appreciate that the first adjective meant "helpless" and the second "zealous." In both cases, there is a clarification by means of extrinsic information. At the lexical level of *Remez*, then, the meaning of a biblical word may be interpreted with reference to its context, other usages in Scripture, or comparative Semitic philology. But if the words of the *Peshat* are translated into another world of discourse, we may learn that the text is "really talking about" a certain philosophical issue, a state of the soul, or the hierarchy of moral qualities. The latter are what Hellenistic writers on allegory called the *hyponoia*, or "deep sense" of the text.

This allegorical aspect of *Remez*, whereby one thing is explained by and in terms of another, shades into a methodological system at the other end of the spectrum. Methodology may thus be perceived as the systematization of a way of coding and coordinating material. The principle of order or arrangement—when external to the text—is the allegory. From this perspective, the truths of interpretation are a function of allegorical structures of the imagination (whether conscious or not). Each allegorical structure is self-contained. The formal difference between the ancient Aramaic Targum's interpretation of the Song of Songs as a history of ancient Israel, and the views of modern commentators who compare its lyrics with the Arabic *wasf* or ancient Egyptian love poems, is that of different points of reference. Both utilize external "figures." In a similar way, the sages of midrash would "interpret (lit., 'release') Scripture (*patar qarya*)" by explicating the words of a text through fixed (though exchangeable) terms of reference.

It is thus evident that each "allegory" is appropriate to the degree that it is judged so by those who share its point of orientation. Shared explorations correct and enlarge one another. They further deepen the community of shared reading in relation to an assumed standard of meaning and method. The text is only known in proportion to the explanative power of any specific allegory—a fact conditioned by cultural taste and requirement. Thus many of the scholarly methodologies of our day satisfy certain historical interests as opposed, say, to other periods of Bible study— when the concern was to understand the text in the light of its religious spirit, or its ethical and ritual imperatives. To bring one type of interpretative allegory into a different cognitive framework, where there is no shared method or meaning, risks miscomprehension and rejection by such labels as "blasphemous" or "unscientific." It therefore makes little sense to compare the ancient rabbinic rules of hermeneutical analogy with modern forms of deductive reasoning—unless one is interested in a comparative history of logic and exegesis. But one might profitably compare the works of the medieval Jewish grammarians (particularly those in the Arab environment) with those of modern students of Semitics; for here the frames of reference are more similar, even if some of the assumptions about language are vastly different.

Taken all together, it should be clear that by *Remez* I mean those hermeneutical strategies whereby meaning is produced for a given text. The *Peshat* is always independent of the *Remez*, to be sure. In Buber's words, "interpretative claims come and go, but the text remains throughout." But we also know that the *Peshat* is in need of the *Remez;* for the text itself maintains a "majestic silence." Without the ever-renewed and necessary allegories of interpretation, the text would not live. Teachers know this truth as task and responsibility. And they seek to transmit it. Analogous to the insight of the rabbis, the written word and the oral teaching (*Peshat* and *Remez*) are the two Torahs of life.

III

Derash is the third level of *PaRDeS*, and includes the tropological and moral spheres of text interpretation. The tropological aspect has traditionally indicated metaphorical and figurative features of a text. For present purposes, we shall not do violence to its concerns if we regard tropology as the sphere of stylistic and compositional considerations. As opposed to the propositional and *extrinsic* accent of the *Remez*, the *Derash* focuses on the positional and *intrinsic* matter of a text.[12] It thus deals with the formal features of the text, and does not go beyond it for clarification.[13]

What is this focus on inner-textual features, and how does it relate to text interpretation? This can be answered by referring to various literary structures which constitute modes of construction within the biblical text. The first of these is the *root* or *word structure*. This corresponds to the "themeword" techniques emphasized by Martin Buber, among others.[14] The repetition of key verbal stems texture a literary pericope in a discernable way. For example, the multiple uses of the word *panim* (face) in Jacob's wrestling scene (Gen. 32:21–32), or *ganav* (steal) in the preceding episode of Rachel's flight (31:19–32) are dramatic cases in point. Similarly, the play and interplay of such words as *qol* (voice), *shamaʿ* (hear), and *maʾas* (despise) determine the theological dynamics and literary ironies found in the story dealing with the sin of Saul in 1 Samuel 15. The root structures are thus constitutive of the *compositional structure* of a text, where the formalities of design and genre are considered. The disruption of such forms, or the integration into larger settings, points to the *editorial structure*. For example, the two narratives in Gen. 3 and 4:1–16 are linked (on a verbal level) and correlated (on a thematic level) by the repetition of materials; while the recurrence of the divine promise of land, seed, and blessing before and after the cycles of the patriarchs (cf. Gen. 12:1–2 and 22:17–18; 26:3–4 and v. 24; 28:3–4 and 35:11–12) integrates these complex epic narratives in the book of Genesis. Moreover, the thematic character of these promises reveal a *motif structure*. Such a structure may combine the components of one text, or it may integrate a series of separate texts. The exodus and eden motifs are cases in point.[15]

Meditation on these structures of *Derash* deepens our aesthetic sensitivity, and introduce us to alternative levels of experience. This brings me to the second aspect of *Derash*, the moral level where a text teaches for the sake of life. To emphasize this point is not to deny that a poem or narrative is often an act of the creative imagination that loves the sound and structure of words. It is rather to direct attention to the effect that these words may have upon us and our being in the world. By the same token, scholarship is not only a matter of facts and methodology. This may have its own appeal, but from the moral perspective of *Derash* scholarship cannot ignore its intergenerational responsibilities as a transmitter of culture. Teachers and scholars thus have a maieutic role as midwives to levels of experience and fact embedded in texts. The moral task of the teacher is to explore modes of textual expression for the sake of a fuller human creativity; while the moral task of the scholar is to recover repressed or forgotten layers of culture for the sake of our fullest human memory. Differently, each unchains the forces of ignorance and repression—in the belief that our *humanitas* is expanded through an encounter with humanity in its historical manifold.

The enhancement of our human being through textual and historical study has a more personal dimension. I mean the attempt to locate the dynamics of the text in one's own experience. At this level of *Derash* the probing hermeneutic strives to go beyond soundings in the archaeology of the imagination, and to intuit a spiritual correspondence between the dynamics of a text and one's own memory. The result, when it happens, is a reciprocal deepening of understanding. The words of a text help to illumine personal experience, and life-experience helps one to penetrate the human issues of a text. Toward this end, the reader must not deny himself, and all that he knows and has experienced. Readiness is all—the readiness to reach out to the text and be reborn. At such moments the text is experienced as revelation.

Let me suggest two examples. The various creation accounts in the Bible are more deeply understood as one strives to encounter their forms and dynamics in a personally engaged way. Indeed, as we try to understand the meaning of 'creation' through its different literary patterns—as calm and cadenced order (Gen. 1–2:4a); as strife and antagonism (Ps. 89:9–11); or as wonder and knowledge (Prov. 8:22–31; Job 38–39)—our own sensibility may be reciprocally expanded. The engaged student thus reads sympathetically out of prior experiences of wonder, resistance, and order; but his capacity is reciprocally enlarged through the new possibilities disclosed by the text. Or to take another case, one may argue that a study of the formal components of prophetic initiations—address, confrontation, resistance, and new speech[16]—are deepened by our human understanding of the confronting power of speech and the experience of resistance to new tasks. Reciprocally, such texts may make us more alive to these dynamics in our personal experience. They thus serve as dialogical partners for reflection, comprehension and growth.

One final dimension of *Derash* in its moral aspect may be noted. By providing a model of engaged reading, a teacher presents himself as one who studies texts within the framework of value and decision. The life-choices and situations embedded in the text are not ignored or neutralized (as generic patterns or abstract structures), but serve as pivots for moral reflection. Teaching is thus more than the transmission of information or even the deepening of the students' humanity. It may also bestow an example of freedom and responsibility.[17]

IV

This brings me, in the end, to *Sod,* the mystical sphere of text interpretation. As noted earlier, many different allegories and teachings attempt to unlock the words of texts. At the mystical level we perceive that just here is their eternal dimension. Each new reading expands the fulness of meanings and extends them in time. The point was already made in antiquity. Starting from Deut. 5:19, which states that at Sinai God spoke "all these words . . . and no more (*velo' yasaph*)," the ancient Targum used the difficult word *yasaph* as a pretext for its deepest concerns, and reread the verse to say that God spoke "without *ceasing.*" There is thus a continual expression of texts; and this reveals itself in their ongoing reinterpretation.

But *Sod* is more than the eternity of interpretation from the human side. It also points to the divine mystery of speech and meaning. Out of silence and separation words create speech-events which provide a habitation for consciousness on earth. But words alone are polyvalent—rife with ambiguities and alternating nuances. For the sake of communication, context and contracted sense are necessary. Social convention thus crowds out creative ambiguity. Poets therefore perform a prophetic task. Breaking the idols of simple sense, they restore the mystery of speech to its transcendent role in the creation of human reality. Teachers may continue this prophetic mission in the service of *Sod.* Mediating a multitude of interpretations, they resist the dogmatization of meaning and the eclipse of the divine lights of speech. From this perspective, the ultimate task of teaching and interpretation is to transcend the idolatries of language. It is a sacred task that condemns hermeneutical arrogance in all its forms—and guards the shrine of speech in the wilderness of power, banality, and desire.

·Conclusion·

THE NOTION OF
A SACRED TEXT

We are no longer as we were. No longer are we sustained within a biblical matrix; or at least not solely so, and not without an acute awareness of competing claims on our spiritual and cognitive integrity. The labor of many centuries has expelled us from this edenic womb and its wellsprings of life and knowledge. And so if essayists like Matthew Arnold and poets like Wallace Stevens have billed the poet as the modern day avatar of priest and rabbi, is this not because the Bible has lost its ancient authority to provide moral guidance and spiritual insight, and to differentiate the sacred and the profane? And further, if modern literary critics still struggle with notions of an integrated text, and such phrases as "sacred text" or "literary canon," are not these too the cultural afterbirth of notions of a sacred Scripture once believed to be a seamless web of integrated meanings?

To be sure, there are those who regard the desacralization of the Bible as the fortunate condition for the rise of new sensibilities and modes of imagination. I will not address this issue here—not because I find it irrelevant or perverse (I do not), but simply because I do not wish to delay discussion of a topic too regularly deferred in modern discourse. What I am concerned with, of course, is the very notion of a sacred text for those of us who do not unreflectingly talk the language of religious tradition, or who cannot—and with whether this notion of a sacred text is at all retrievable at this historical hour.

Since this question affects our innermost cultural being, and traces our relationship to the foundational text of our religious and cultural origins, there is no choice but to speak personally. This choice is reinforced by my deep conviction that genuine questions are those that seize us and from which there can be no honest evasion. In this respect I am very much a disciple of Franz Rosenzweig. But how can this notion of a sacred text be encountered—given our present alienation from such matters and the fact that we come to this topic through a mix of modern notions regarding texts, their status, and the role of a reader? I have no unilateral solution, and offer no simple procedure. By way of one possibility, I shall try here first to think my way back into older configurations of this topic in Jewish literature. In this way, I hope to align my concern with premodern possibilities and to reshape my all-too-modern sensibilities through them. I shall then confront this historical achievement with a series of concerns which are very much part of the contemporary critical temper. From this dialectical conjunction, a personal synthesis will then be offered—an attempt to retrieve the notion of a sacred text for myself, today. I share it out of a desire to prolong—even provoke—discourse on this topic, and thus to retrieve it as a matter of collective concern.

I

During the more than one thousand year history of ancient Israelite culture, countless historical traditions were sifted, blended, and refocused, and countless teachings were scrutinized, supplemented, and winnowed. The result, derived from different groups and ideologies, was the Hebrew Bible: a complex anthology of teachings and memories. Coordinating these multiple and frequently conflicting vectors are three principle realities: the divine will, the human teacher, and the community of faith. The divine will is, of course, the axial point in this triad. For the divine will is, within the Hebrew Bible, the source of all teachings, value, and sacrality. Since, on this world view, the world and mankind have no sources of sacrality in and of themselves, they are radically dependent upon divine teachings, as mediated by the formative and ongoing teachers of Israel. With time, the historical personage of Moses became the point of convergence of many teachings and their revision. And insofar as Moses was renowned as a principal conduit of divine teachings to the community, the dicta reported in Moses' name assumed divine authority. Many other teachers—prophets, wisemen, and priests—arose to instruct the people and transmit or integrate the sacred tradition. Recognizing this diversity of teachers, and the diverse authority of their instructions, early generations of rabbinic sages established pedigrees of revelation and inspiration among the received biblical texts, and plotted these latter according to such criteria.

It is thus that the traditions and teachings which compose the Hebrew Bible constitute the world of meanings of the communities and spokesmen of ancient Israel. And the language whereby these traditions and teachings were formulated became the shaper of discourse, praxis, and imagination for the culture. Certainly this was the case when these matters were orally taught and transmitted; and it became all the more so when the teachings and traditions of Israel were transformed into a closed, written text. For through such closure the fluid and historically variable teachings preserved by different circles and parties—teachings which naturally promoted and supported varieties of theological and social concerns—became the inviolate record of divine speech and action. Inevitably, all who laid claim to the sacred traditions of Israel laid claim to this closed deposit as to the sole repository of all sacred performance and possibility. Contestations therefore developed not so much over the written record as over its evaluation, status, and exegetical meaning. This factor clearly marks the formation of ancient Judaism, and pulses explicitly and implicitly through all the documents known from two centuries (and more) prior to the onset of the common era, and for two centuries (and more) thereafter.

For classical Judaism, then, the notion of sacrality which adheres to the biblical text by virtue of its source in divinity was gradually protected, qualified, and even extended by hermeneutical systems which reopened the closed text. This led to paradox after paradox until, remarkably, the very sanctity of biblically derived actions hung by hermeneutical threads of one length or another, and until the very sanctity of the biblical text was itself hermeneutically established. Thus by virtue of its famous myth of two Torahs—the one written and the other oral, but both given coterminously at Sinai—the Pharasaic sages laid claim to the true chain of interpretation whereby the written Torah was to be historically renewed.[1] Those who interpreted differently were excluded from intimate religious fellowship: for they did not disclose the inherent—divinely concealed—sanctity of Scripture as safeguarded by Pharasaic hermeneutics. And further, this very same Pharasaic hermeneutical tradition reciprocally established new criteria for the sanctity of the biblical text—transferring to its physical state hermeneutically established notions of priestly contagion. Thus the Pharasaic expression "to defile the hands" is the technical phrase for an inspired, sacred text.[2] Arguably, this designation also served polemical, exclusionary purposes—specifically against the Sadducees.

There are other paradoxes and developments which must be briefly noted before we leave this classical rabbinic matrix. First, the emergence of a fullblown exegetical system necessarily deepened the sacral possibilities of the received biblical corpus. This was partly achieved through the effacement of the boundaries which ostensibly distinguished biblical books, boundaries consisting in differences in their contents and their authority. Gradually, a perceived anthological unity of the canon displaced the received disunity and diversity of its contents. Separate texts could not be rigidly set off from each other; and their common, canonical sacrality meant that the divine attributions of some texts inevitably affected the status and evaluation of others. For example, the existence of a divinely sponsored Torah in one section of Scripture eventually affected literary deposits of human wisdom lying elsewhere—with the result that the authority and higher sacrality of the one lead to the reinterpretation of the other. Thus the canonical consociation of the Pentateuch and the Book of Proverbs was a major factor in the readiness of classical Judaism to perceive the Torah as both grounded in and an expression of Wisdom. Indeed, without this canonical link the significant Platonic influence on classical and later Judaism is virtually incomprehensible.

At another level, the effacement of the formal boundaries between canonical books and their contents went yet further, and allowed the potential plurivocity of sacred Scripture to be explored. Indeed, once the surface sequence of words, sentences, and pericopae were no longer solely determinate of textual meaning, complex networks of intertextuality were established. In the words of a justly famous dictum: "There is no anteriority or posteriority in Scripture."[3] From a literary-critical perspective, this rabbinic utterance meant that all elements in the received text were the indeterminate components of a closed semiotic field. By the normative hermeneutical rules of the game, new combinations of words and texts—hence, new meanings—were thus endlessly possible. From a theological perspective, this dictum also indicated that the biblical text was a special expression of divine fulness for a community of faith willing to extract its sacral possibilities. From both viewpoints, then, it is clear that the common observation that the halakhic process is exoteric in nature is hardly sufficient. It is, of course, true (and remains so) that halakhic teachings are public and not secret. But it remains to be stressed that for the rabbis of the Law, no less than for contemporary allegorists and mystics, exegesis involved the decoding of hidden networks of biblical meaning. They, too, were concerned to render the implicit teachings of the Sinaitic revelation explicit for each generation. What the mystical esotericists did was to descend even further into the hidden mysteries of Scripture to that point where the essence of the Bible and the *deus revelatus* were One. Hereby, the sacrality of the biblical text actually merged with the sacrality of the Godhead. The Bible was not so much a revelation of the divine will, as a revelation of the divine Being—in all its unfathomable depths.

Certainly one of the great contributions of Judaism to the history of religions is its assertion that the divine reality makes itself humanly comprehensible through the structures of language. Restated from the mundane perspective of Rabbi Ishmael, the divine infinity is formulated—we may say, humanized—by conventional human language.[4] When viewed, however, from the supramundane perspective which developed in Jewish mysticism, the humanly communicable language inscribed in Scripture is but a reflex of the divine infinity. It is but the outer garment, so to speak, of the eternal feminine within God that draws us erotically—platonically, and with religious ardor—into the consummate depths of God. Mystical hermeneutics are thus part of a sacred ritual which allows the adept to rise through the orders of divine being hidden within Scripture toward the divine reality which reverberates throughout all the worlds. Indeed, as Rabbi Simeon bar Yochai, the pseudepigraphic author of the *Zohar*, daringly observed, the surface level of scriptural meaning is of such little account that the literature of the nations exceed it in stylistic and literary splendor. For one who knows how to read, he added, the surface sense of the Bible is simply the lowest rung on the ladder of mystical ascension.[5] This idea was variously elaborated upon in Jewish mystical literature. Viewed compositely, it was taught that the biblical text was merely the mundane exteriorization of at least three fundamental divine truths. First, the language of Scripture is a coded expression of the very structure of the Godhead in all its dynamic energy and syntheses. Second, the language of Scripture is nothing less than the condensed earthly form of divine speech which descends throughout all the worlds, and which has many levels of meaning at every station thereof.[6] In mystical truth, following the formulation of Moses Cordovero, the four principal worlds of the divine emanation are filled with infinite worlds where the Torah is variously read and comprehended in accordance with the power of comprehension of the beings in every one of them.[7] Hereby, the sacrality of Scripture lies in its emergence from the infinitely pregnant divine Logos, and in its capacity to restore the mystical adept to the transcendent sacrality of the Godhead. Inversely stated, an even more powerful implication may be drawn from all this: namely, that whatever can be humanly known of God is not fixed but only that which we can interpret about Him through Scripture.

My third point complements this latter one, yet takes one unexpected turn. According to kabbalistic teachings, the surface language of Scripture is nothing less than the ineffable Name of God, the Tetragrammaton.[8] At one level, this teaching is comparable to those concerning the divine Logos, since it would be accurate to say that all of Scripture is a coded formulation of the Tetragrammaton in all its infinite and symbolic transformations. Otherwise put, the sacrality of Scripture lies in its being a readable, semantic arrangement of the mysteries of the Tetragrammaton in a document meant for the public realm. But there is more to it than that. Since the Tetragrammaton is the very essence of the Godhead, the sacrality of Scripture also partakes of the sacrality of God. However, since the Tetragrammaton in Scripture is truly ineffable, the Torah as divine Name has nothing to do with the mundane communicative or social functions of a name. It is rather an expression of the belief that God has been able to express—better, compress—His transcendent splendor in and through the creation. The holy Name thus represents the concentrated power of God in the world and in Scripture. From this perspective, the sacrality of Scripture is neither derived nor attributed: it is rather a sacrality which partakes of the very essence of God. So conceived, God is not only present through Scripture, He is in it as well.

II

My preceding remarks echo the four fold levels of scriptural meaning as developed in rabbinic Judaism.[9] The first level was that of the plain-sense meaning of the text, within the ancient Israelite communities of faith. The second level touched on hermeneutical developments of that text within subsequent communities with different ideological and social concerns. The third dealt with the symbolic structure of the text as a protean form within which new, hidden meanings could be found. And the fourth level of the biblical text was its transcendent dimension—its deep divine affinities, even identities. As noted, each of these levels generated its own type of sacrality. Accordingly, the traditional sacrality of the Bible is at once simple and symbolic, individual and communal, practical and paradoxical. But times have changed, and with them the temper of interpretation.

To begin, let me note that in modern criticism the formal boundaries of a text and its interpretation are opened infinitely. There are no shared rules of interpretation, and no one interpretation fundamentally precludes any other. At the very least, this simple fact means that the interpretation of a text neither derives from nor leads to a common world of value or discourse. Interpretations are as varied as their interpreters. For if there are no shared rules of interpretation the Archimedean point is the autonomous interpreter himself, and his relative notions of reading and value. The text is thus no heteronomous presence; no *objectivum* for the interpreter. Instead, the text is nothing without him—the imperious interpreter—who not only establishes meaning through interpretation but, if we follow certain critics, actually establishes the text itself by his interpretation. Not consciously, I trust, parodying the mystical metaphor of textual garments and layers of meaning, Roland Barthes actually spoke of the text as an onion which the interpreter peels. But, you will note, the onion is nothing but its layers; and so when all of them are peeled, there is no onion. All that remains is the interpreter.

With the absence of a transcendent or transcendental Archimedean point of reference, we may now add, the biblical text is thoroughly disenfranchised from its sacred ground. There is no will-to-meaning inherent in the text which awaits the patient interpreter. There is only the solitary will-to-power of the interpreter who regally reads and establishes meaning. No releaser is he. He is instead the maker of meanings, the marker of contradictions, the mandrake who fertilizes the barren textual field. All this, of course, has serious consequences. It may result in the exciting competition of methodologies in which various strategies of reading and textual reconstruction are debated. For just how the exegetically disclosed fragments should be diachronically evaluated and aligned is of obvious hermeneutical concern—particularly so with the Bible, since its evaluation has been historicized, and its varieties and contradictions cannot be resolved synchronically. At another level, a whole series of evasions arises in order to outflank the relative voice of the interpreter and establish objective features of critical inquiry. And then there is the whole question of whether and how modern criticism should establish its moral ground.

All these are important issues. And if in some ways the greatness of our classical texts is lost or somewhat eclipsed in the process, we earnestly recognize that these texts are also pretexts for new ways of talking in the public realm, of defining strategies of analysis, and of establishing moral and methodological guidelines (which bear as much on living as on reading and interpreting). The plurivocity of the text—and here we specifically mean the biblical text—has thus been displaced by the plurivocity of many autonomous readers and interpreters. On the one hand, this is our solidarity as readers; but on the other it is also our solitariness as persons who appropriate texts rather than being appropriated by them—as it once was in the past.

And yet this is not altogether the case; for there is a domain acknowledged by modern criticism where we, as readers, are duly appropriated—one might say, constituted—by texts. What I have in mind is the well-known structuralist concept of *intertextualité,* which is concerned with the relationship of any one text to others. Or, in the words of Julia Kristeva, "every text is the absorption and transformation of other texts. The notion of intertextuality comes to take the place of the notion of intersubjectivity."[10] At first glance this may seem but a substitution of the dictum "there are no texts, only relations between them" for "there are no texts, only readers." But this is not entirely the case. For as Jonathan Culler, in his comments on Kristeva's remarks, notes, "intersubjectivity—the shared knowledge which is applied in reading—is a function of these other texts (which provide the grid through which the one text is read and structured). . . . Though it is difficult to discover the sources of all the notions . . . which make up the 'I' of the reader, subjectivity is not so much a personal core as intersubjectivity, the track or furrow left by texts of all kinds."[11] To rephrase the matter, one may say that we are constituted—even appropriated—by the texts we read. They are our interior Tower of Babel, filling us with the many voices of the many texts that make us who we are. And if today there is no necessary or expectable echo between the way we are inhabited by texts and the way we live thereby, then our private integrations of texts constitute us now this way, now that, but always separately and always relative to our emotional, spiritual, and hermeneutical maturity.

So much is clear enough. What remains is to point out the bearing this has on the sacrality of texts, and the difficulty of retrieving this notion now. First of all, the intertextuality of a given sacred text—say, any one text in the Bible—is no longer circumscribed by its canonical cohorts. Reference points are no longer solely intracanonical. Now, we feel, all texts should be available for the interpreters who coordinate these many texts for interpretation; and also that these many texts are constantly rehierarchized as our values and life tasks change. We thus live with texts and fragments of texts, in myriad and fluid groupings.

For a text like the Bible, then, we come to realize that its literary and even spiritual aspects are not engaged differently from those of a novel or poem. Indeed, the Bible does not address us in its entirety, but as a canon-within-a-canon—as a selected cluster of texts or fragments which live within us amid many other, non-biblical clusters. To put it bluntly, I daresay that we value the love lyrics of the Song of Songs more than the deuteronomic laws of extermination; the images of spiritual inclusion more than the laws of national exclusion; and so on. We choose. In fact, we must admit that our moral and spiritual vision may be only partly derived from the Bible; and that our biblical values are not inevitably the measure whereby these fragments are constituted within us, or achieve whatever sacrality they may. Our eyes wander to other visions, and our hearts often reject the words of Moses—and this we proudly attribute to our spiritual development or moral maturity. Who will deny it?

III

All this said, let me now pose the question that has been in my heart all along. Can the notion of a sacred text be retrieved? Indeed, is the notion of a sacred Scripture at all retrievable in an age of desacralization and dehierarchization; in an age of atrocity and disenfranchisement; and in an age where a text can be reduced to a microfiche or floppy disc? Possibly; and to mark this possibility I shall retrace the four fold structure of textual sanctity discussed earlier—only in reverse.

As suggested earlier, it is arguably one of Judaism's greatest contributions to the history of religions to assert that the divine Reality is communicated to mankind through words. The literary form in which this is realized is, of course, the Bible. In it we have our culturally paradigmatic expression of the fateful crossing from the ineffable and infinite plenitude of God to the wholly effable and finite features of human language. I say paradigmatic—for the Bible is but our particular cultural prism for the linguistic crossing which occurs every time silence is broken by speech, and reality is verbalized. The divine pleroma which comes to expression through the spoken breath of mankind is thus our triumph and our poverty. It is our triumph because it asserts our link to divinity—our opportunity to domesticate that infinity through the imagination. But speech is our poverty as well. For our mortal desires contract God's infinity and upset majestic intricacies. Through our all-too-human mirror, the divine light is glazed by neurosis and tarnished by smallmindedness.

Put differently, our hermeneutical hope is in the indissoluble link between the divine and human *textus*—the divine *textus* being the texture of truth as it converges upon itself, and the human *textus* being our rationalized versions of this divine texture in culture. On the other side, our existential poverty is our unawareness of this link, and our exegetical proclivity to cross over too fast from the one *textus* to the other. Too soon do we close the terrifying gap between the divine infinity and a human world of words; too incautiously do we transform the *mysterium tremendum* into the *fascinosum* of social celebrations and familiarity.

It is at such points that the ancient theophanic power of illimitable divinity may yet break through swollen words—like the raging waters of the depths that may pierce the ice-encrusted sea, as the poet Bialik imagined. Surely we know the erupting force of new poems upon our imagination. May we also not recognize in the Bible—the foundational document of our culture—an exemplary expression of this process? Repeatedly do the prophets protest false images of divinely-given reality; and strongly does Job dismantle the deuteronomic rationalizations of divine involvement with the world. Indeed, Job speaks with a prophetic voice. He is a destroyer of self-serving visions for the sake of a more honest crossing from the divine *textus* to the human one. Through Job's insistence, and the Voice from the whirlwind which decenters his intellectual pretensions as well, the divine *textus* is imagined. Now the human hermeneutical impulse, and the culture-building strategies of smallminded man, are broken. Now the divine intervenes. As of old, sacredness erupts through a confrontation with the Presence of God—a numinous moment that transcends interpretation and representation in every possible way.

Thus, in a first move, we may say that the Bible itself may help to retrieve the notion of a sacred text—insofar as it is emblematic of the necessary cross-over from the one *textus* to the other; and insofar as it

retains all those theophanic-prophetic eruptions which mock our desire
to "write"—in Emerson's words—"the order of the variable winds." Indeed the task of crossing over from one realm to the other is revealed
through the Bible as the burden of a spiritually conscious existence.
Father Abraham is our model here, for he is the first *Ivri*—the first one in
our culture to "cross over" from the divine infinity to historical existence
and its risks.[12] He is our great *Ivri*, our heroic Crosser, and thus utterly
different from Jonah who calls himself an *Ivri* but fears the consequences
of speech in the human *textus*.

The Bible thus dramatizes the linkage between the human and divine
textus, and expresses the hopes and terrors of this necessity. It is, in truth,
the Book of the *Ivrim*: the Book of the Over-crossers.

Another possible level of textual sacrality lies in the capacity of the Bible
to incorporate multiple structures of reality. On the one hand, the literature of ancient Israel reveals the contestation of diverse proponents of the
truth of Yahwism, and its practical implementation. It is also obvious,
however, that the closure of Scripture has left the inheritors of this
anthology with one text and many contending claims of meaning and
purpose. Some saw the proper actualization of the Hebrew Bible in *nomos*,
others in prophecy; but all invariably claimed to be the true heirs of
ancient Israel, exclusively fit (by God and exegetical grace) to explicate the
fulness of the written inheritance.

This contestation was no shadow play, by any means, but conducted in
deathly earnest. Indeed where one "Truth" is proclaimed or revealed, as
in the Western monotheistic religions, the rivalry to be *the* authentic
witness to that truth is the sad historical fact. The outsider has been
peremptorily hounded, excluded, and ejected. While a dismal fact, the
underlying reality seems darker yet. For one of the most profoundly
disturbing aspects of the work of Otto Rank and Ernest Becker, his
contemporary disciple, is that all ideologies are at bottom immortality
systems: cognitive and ritually supported structures which establish the
individual's or community's being-in-the-world and justify their link with
past and future generations.[13] In short, ideologies and symbol systems establish one's death-denying and death-transcending claim: a claim which
excludes the outsider and contends for the right to rank or divide the
resources of this world. Accordingly, on this view of human nature—
of which I am largely persuaded—ideological confrontations, religious
wars, and contestations of truth and value are inevitable. We mark off
duration within the earthly realm through high cognitive investments in
our symbolic maps of reality. That the root of this deep human divisive-
ness is largely unconscious, and acted out with all sorts of evasive and
moralizing rationalizations, makes the matter all the more insidious.

To my mind, this overall anthropology provides a paradoxical perspective on the schemas of sacrality found in Scripture—and among its inheritors. For if the Bible is a text rife with competing immortality systems, *in and through* these very contestations a prophetic voice may be heard. What I mean is this: Just as the Bible is characterized by prophetic instructions and critiques (which alternatively sponsor and shatter exclusive visions), the entire text may be regarded as a prophetic eruption in its own right. Indeed if we look at the competing symbolic systems from the perspective of human attempts to live with divinity, and to transcend the specter of death, then the Bible provides a textual microcosm of our human-religious travail. It may thus enable us to achieve some critical and compassionate distance from it, and even help neutralize the competing claims of inner-biblical and post-biblical ideologies. A hint of this hope may be found in the Bible itself—in Micah's reinterpretation of Isaiah's prophecy. The latter envisioned an era of peace in which all nations would go to Zion to be instructed by the God of Israel (Isa. 2:1–4). The prophet Micah received this tradition intact, but added one revolutionary coda to it: that each nation, Israel included, would go in the name of its own god (Mic. 4:5). Translated into modern terms, one may say that Micah foresaw the multiple visions of peace of all peoples as converging toward a truth which Israel knows through its God. No symbolic construction would exclude any other in this vision of "concordant discord."

The upshot of these reflections is to suggest a new type of sacredness sponsored by the Bible: not the sacredness of the raging, exclusive vision, but the sacredness of the chastened, inclusive one. Such a vision would provide an opening to transcendence not by demoting other symbolic models but by seeing in the Bible a model for a plurality of visions of multiform humanity. The sacrality released hereby would not be the competitive sacrality of segregated symbols. Rather, this new Bible-sponsored sacrality would allow the awesome transcendence of the divine reality to chasten our constructions of order and sacrality. And if you should say that this is naive, and ignores the harsh wisdom of Rank and Becker noted earlier, then know that I take my clue from Becker himself. For Becker, acknowledging the inescapable conclusions of his anthropological analysis, has no illusions that our human condition will fundamentally change. But he does grant to sociology the critical voice of the moral adversary: the voice that keeps humanity aware of its inherent tendencies as death-denying symbolizers.[14] I would propose a similar task for the Bible. Just as the Hebrew Bible was the original cultural sponsor of raging differences, so may it now sponsor the eruption of a prophetic voice: critical of the potential dangers of human symbolic systems, and an advocate for their fragility and plurality. So perceived, the Bible relativizes the idols of the human *textus* for the sake of the divine *textus;* and it points to that sphere where our death is not transcended symbolically, but is absorbed into the fulness of God.

IV

Having now passed through three of the four textual levels mentioned earlier—the theological, the hermeneutical, and the symbolic—I turn to the level where the text communicates its plain-sense to a community. What may this mean now? Is there a sacral possibility hidden here for those who acknowledge the determinant position of the Bible in our culture, but have been deeply affected by the conditions that have widened the chasm between persons and texts? I shall focus on two poles of concern. The first starts with the private realm, where an individual reads texts in a wholly personal manner—initially separate from communal discourse. Here, we may say, modern readers prowl around texts like wolves around Sinai—to paraphrase Kafka's well-known parable. Indeed we prowl around many texts, the Bible included, and wrest from these encounters fragments of various sorts. So viewed, we are, in part, a living texture of ideas derived from our reading—centering points of multiple texts which constitute our interior and exterior worlds. Accordingly, the Bible may become sacred to us insofar as its images and language shape our discourse, stimulate our moral and spiritual growth, and simply bind us to past generations which also took this text seriously. Indeed, the Bible may become sacred in this way because—together with other texts—it helps establish our personhood and outline our possibilities; and because it may provide the words and values through which we may cross over from the private to the interhuman realm. No denial of death is this. It is rather a transcending of selfhood and its limitations through concourse with other texts and other selves.

My second pole of concern begins in the public realm, where every sharing of textual fragments is a sharing in the common human world. Private readings may thus promote shared speech and so new moral opportunities—which returns me to the beginning of my meditations. I then spoke of the transcendent capacity of the Bible to disclose the divine Reality. We now come to the same point from another side. For what is shared when persons communicate their private world of textual fragments? Is it not a realization of the partiality of every attempt to decode divine truth? Shared speech thus discloses new versions of the sacred, but prophetically chastens them as well. Our fragmentary interpretations are not final: other readers will inevitably rescue a different sense from Sinai.

"The voice of the Lord is in strength," says Scripture (Ps. 29:4); and the rabbinic sages added—in the strength of each person's understanding.[15]

Perhaps, we imagine, it is in the transcendental convergence of all interpretations—literary as well as personal—that the divine Reality may be approximated. Or is this our supreme fiction in a Bible-sponsored culture, which asserts that verbal images may purchase truth? If so, the ultimate sacral possibility of the Bible may then lie in its capacity to reprove the very pretensions to meaning through language which it has itself sponsored. So viewed, the transcendent sacrality of the Bible is more than a vision of a transcendent divine fulness prior to speech. It may rather lie in teaching that God's truth transcends all linguistic pretensions to meaning. By this rule, the Bible itself, with its own pretension to present a humanly conditioned divine voice, would also be radically transcended. Here, I suggest, is the final prophetic voice of the text. Or is it the divine voice which speaks to Job, and asks: Do you love God more than tradition, more than all your versions of the sacred?

NOTES

1. Inner-Biblical Exegesis

1. For the rabbinic image of God as a scholar of Torah, see *b. Berakhot* 8b, 63b, and *b. Avodah Zarah* 3b.

2. *M. Avot* I, 1 and parallels, on which now see M. Herr, "Continuum in the Chain of Transmission," *Zion* 44 (1979), 43–56 (in Hebrew).

3. The strongest argument for formal and terminological external influence has been made by D. Daube, "Rabbinic Methods of Interpretation and Hellenistic Rhetoric," *Hebrew Union College Annual* 22 (1949), 239–65, and "Alexandrian Methods of Interpretations and the Rabbis," *Festschrift H. Lewald* (Basel: Helbing and Lichtenholm, 1953), 27–44. S. Lieberman, *Hellenism in Jewish Palestine* (New York: Jewish Theological Seminary, 1962), pp. 56–68, has denied a genetic influence and restricted the borrowing to terminology. We cannot pursue the matter here.

4. Much of the ensuing discussion draws upon my *Biblical Interpretation in Ancient Israel* (Oxford: Clarendon Press, 1985), hereinafter *BIAI*. The interested reader may find there a much fuller range of textual examples and conceptual analyses. I have not at all considered the reinterpretation of prophecies in this essay; for this see *BIAI*, pt. 4.

5. See, for example, G. Fohrer, "Tradition und Interpretation in Alten Testament," *Zeitschrift für die alttestamentlischer Wissenschaft* 73 (1961), 1–30.

6. This observation was already made by Ibn Ezra.

7. See also *BIAI*, pp. 48–49, and n. 15 there.

8. Already S. D. Luzzatto, *Il Propheta Isaia, volgarizzate e commentato* (Padua: A. Bianchi, 1855), pp. 337–38.

9. See H. W. Hertzberg, "Die Nachgeschichte alttestamentlicher Texte innerhalb des Alten Testament," in *Werden und Wesen des Alten Testaments,* ed. P. Volz, F. Stummer, and J. Hempel (BZAW 66; Berlin: Töpelman, 1936), p. 114.

10. See I. L. Seligmann, *The Septuagint Version of Isaiah: A Discussion of Its Problems* (Mededeelingen en Verhandeelingen het Vooraziatisch-Egyplisch Genootschap "Ex Oriente Lux," I; Leiden: E. J. Brill, 1948), p. 19.

11. Cf. *BIAI*, pp. 89–95.

12. Ibid., pp. 60–62.

13. Ibid., pp. 187–97.

14. For the view that the Hebrew phrase *al tis'u* means "do not barter," see C. Tchernowitz, *Toledot ha-Halakhah* (New York, 1945–53), 3:113–17; but see my criticism, *BIAI*, p. 132 n. 73.

15. Note the more explicit language in Neh. 13:15–16, which is based on this Jeremian text.

16. See *BIAI*, pt. 3.

17. Or "bear the responsibility/penalty"; cf. W. Zimmerli's analysis of the idiom *ns' 'wn* in "Die Eigenart der prophetischen Reden des Ezechiel: Ein Beitrag zum Problem an Hand von Ez. 14:1–11," *ZAW* 66 (1954), 8–12. The following *ashmah* is thus used in a consequential sense, in addition to the more general sense of legal "guilt" (as commonly in biblical Hebrew for this and related terms).

18. Cf. Jer. 30:16.

19. Possibly read *mizbeah*, "slaughter-site," for *zebah*, "slaughter." Cf. the parallelism in Hos. 10:1–2.

20. Cf., for example, the revision of 1 Kings 8:25 in 2 Chron. 6:16.

21. For an analysis with examples, see *BIAI*, pp. 247–54, 425–28.

22. Overall, see ibid., pp. 528–42.

23. See my discussion in "Form and Formulation of the Biblical Priestly Blessing," *Journal of the American Oriental Society* 103.1 (1983), 115–21.

2. Extra-Biblical Exegesis

1. See *Sifrei Deuteronomy*, ed. L. Finkelstein, p. 423; also *Avot de-Rabbi Natan*, B, ch. 46, ed. S. Schechter, 65a, and *yer. Ta 'anit* iv. 2. 68a.

2. For the reading "one reading" and "another (reading)," emending *bi-derash ehad* and *bi-derash aher* to *bi-derekh ehad* and *bi-derekh aher*, respectively, see S. Lieberman, *Hellenism in Jewish Palestine* (New York: Jewish Theological Seminary, 1962), 21 n. 9.

3. For an overall introduction to the *qeri-ketiv* phenomenon, see the discussion of C. D. Ginsburg, *Introduction to the Massoretico-Critical Edition of the Hebrew Bible* (1897), pt. II, chap. vii; also chap. xi (iii–iv). This work has been reprinted with a critical prolegomenon by H. Orlinsky (New York: Ktav Publishing House, 1966). For a critique of earlier views, and a fresh proposal, see J. Barr, "A New Look at Ketibh-Qere," *Oudtestamentische Studiën* 21 (1981), 19–37.

4. In addition to this phrase, cf. the equivalent expression *ve-'adayin ha-dabar talui* in *Sifrei Deuteronomy*, ed. Finkelstein, p. 393. On the more complicated idiom *ve'ad akhshav ha-moznayim me'uyin* ("and thus far the scales are balanced"), see *Tanhuma, Ki Tissa'* 34; also cf. *Tanhuma* Buber, *Shelah*, Add. from Ms. Rome 39b–40a.

5. In the remark "Perhaps *ibbaneh* from her" there is a play on the verb *banah* (to build) and the noun *ben* (son). One can understand *ibbaneh* to mean "I shall be built up" *and* "I shall be provided a son."

6. See the discussion of E. Y. Kutscher, *Ha-Lashon Ve-Hareqa' Ha-Leshoni Shel Megillat Yeshayah* (Jerusalem: Magnes Press, 1959), 171. There are many other cases were the vowel *qametz qaton* is marked by a *vav* at Qumran. A Massoretic parallel occurs at Jer. 1:5. The traditional *ketiv* for "I created you" is *etzarekha*, while the *qeri* is *etzorekha*—with a *vav* used to mark the second vowel. Medieval speculations to the contrary (Rashi and R. Joseph Kara construed the *qeri* from the stem *tzur* (to circumscribe), it would seem that the *qeri-ketiv* variants here are simply orthographic alternatives of the same verbal stem *yatzar* (to create).

7. See the compendium and discussion of A. Rosenzweig, "Die Al-Tikrei Deutungen," *Festschrift . . . I. Lewy* (Breslau, 1911), 204–53. A rich range of examples may be culled from the often remarkable (traditional) study of R. Samuel Waldberg, *Sepher Darkhei Ha-Shinnuyim* (Lemberg, 1870; reprint, Jerusalem: Makor, 1970). My thanks to Professor David Weiss Halivni for this reference and for providing me with a copy.

8. See H. Strack, *Talmud Babylonicum cod. Monacensis,* 95 (Leiden, 1912), fol. 71b.

9. See his *Commentary on the Sefer Yetzirah* (Berlin: Z. H. Itzkovski, 1885), 23.

10. For a striking use of Prov. 27:26 in connection with *sitrei torah,* see *Song of Songs Rabba* I. i. 2.

11. See *Major Trends in Jewish Mysticism* (New York: Schocken Books, paper ed., 1961), 31.

12. *On the Kabbalah and Its Symbolism* (New York: Schocken Books, 1965), 121.

13. Ibid., 121f.

14. See Mandelbaum, ed., II, 379–81, for the text.

15. Greek *dynamis* here translates Hebrew *gevurah.* Cf. the wide-ranging discussion of E. E. Urbach, *The Sages* (Jerusalem: Magnes Press, 1969), ch. 5 (Hebrew).

16. See Targum Ps.-Jonathan I, *ad loc.;* and the tradition in *Yalqut Shim'oni, Ve'ethanan* 814.

17. For an analysis of the divine power who figures in this passage, see G. Scholem, *Jewish Gnosticism, Merkabah Mysticism, and Talmudic Tradition* (New York: Jewish Theological Seminary, 1965), 51–55; and for a striking prayer of the type suggested by our passage, see M. Cohen, *The Shi'ur Qomah* (Landham, MD: University Press of America, 1983), 246, ll. 182–85.

18. More precise speculations regarding the occasion of this discourse are offered by A. Goldberg in *Qiryat Sefer* 43 (1967–68), 77.

19. "*kivyakhol,*" in J. J. Kobak's *Jeschurun* 4 (1871), 1–6.

20. *Die exegetische Terminologie der jüdischen Traditionsliteratur* (Leipzig, 1899), I, 72.

21. A. Marmorstein, *The Old Rabbinic Doctrine of God. II. Essays in Anthropomorphism* (London, 1937; reprint, New York: KTAV, 1968), 131, recognized that *kivyakhol* is no mere disclaimer for rabbinic anthropomorphisms, and that it is found near scriptural passages. But he left the point hanging and, in a sense, ambiguous. In addition, his fanciful explanation of the term as an acronym thoroughly blurred a precise appreciation of the dynamics at hand.

22. See *Megillat Ha-Miqdash,* ed. Y. Yadin (Jerusalem, 1977), I: 285–90, II: 202–04. The particular construction found there, where the *vav* of (*vehumat*) *vetalita* is understood as explicative (viz., "and you shall hang him on a tree, *that* he die") is also preserved in the beraitha at *b. Sanhedrin* 46b, and in textual readings found in the Peshitta and some manuscripts of the Septuagint. On these readings, see M. Wilcox, "'Upon the Tree'—Deut. 21:22–23 in the New Testament," *Journal of Biblical Literature* 96 (1977), 90, and L. Rosso, "Deuteronomio 21, 22. Contributo del Rotolo del Tempio Alla Valutazione di una Variante Medievale dei Settanta," *Revue de Qumran* 9 (1977), 231–36.

23. In the edition of H. S. Horovitz, *Siphre D'Be Rab* (Leipzig, 1917; reprint, Jerusalem: Wahrmann Books, 1966), 81f.

24. On this, cf. Ginsburg, *op. cit.,* 347–67. For early examples of this phenomenon in the Bible, see my *Biblical Interpretation in Ancient Israel* (Oxford: The Clarendon Press, 1985), 66–77.

25. For this phenomenon, see H. Weiner, *The Composition of Judges II 11 to 1 Kings II 46* (Leipzig: J. C. Hinrichs, 1929); and C. Kuhl, "Die 'Wiederaufnahme'— ein literarisches Prinzip?," *Zeitschrift für die alttestamentlicher Wissenschaft* 64 (1952), 1–11.

26. For an even stronger conclusion, see W. E. Barnes, "Ancient Corrections in the Text of the Old Testament (*Tikkun Sopherim*)," *Journal of Theological Studies* 1 (1900), 413: "the *tikkun* tradition is not Massoretic (i.e. textual) but Midrashic (i.e. exegetical or, more accurately, homiletic)." This position is rejected by Lieberman, *op. cit.,* 28–37.

27. See the observations of M. Gudëmann, *Religionsgeschichtliche Studien* (Leipzig, 1876), 26ff., and B. Heller, "Die Saga von Sarge Josephs . . . ," *Monatschrift für die Geschichte und Wissenschaft des Judentums* 70 (1926), 271ff.

28. For an examination of the textual and recensional variants of this text with an eye to their treatment of the "magical" content involved, see J. Goldin, "The Magic of Magic and Superstition," in *Aspects of Religious Propaganda in Judaism and Early Christianity*, ed. E. Schüssler-Fiorenza, (Notre Dame: University of Notre Dame Press, 1976), 127f. (and notes).

3. The Garments of Torah

1. Translation from G. Scholem, ed., *Zohar—The Book of Splendor: Basic Readings from the Kabbalah* (New York: Schocken Books, 1963), 121f. The esoteric distinction between the "body" and "soul" of a text, and the notion that the outer sense is a "garment" for the inner one, even appears in commentators who are not mystical in any way. See, for example, the couplets in R. Abraham ibn Ezra's introduction to Lamentations, or the comment of Don Isaac Abarbanel to Gen. 2:4.

2. Cf. E. Benveniste, "Les Relations de temps dans le verbe francais," in his *Problemes de linguistique generale* (Paris: Gallimard, 1966), 237–50.

3. See the discussion in S. Lieberman, *Hellenism in Jewish Palestine* (New York: Jewish Theological Seminary, 1962), 106–110.

4. Texts and discussion in S. Lieman, *The Canonization of Hebrew Scripture* (Hamden, CT: Archon Books, 1976), 102–20.

5. An aspect of this theme is discussed below.

6. Cf. H. Hagendahl, *Augustine and the Latin Classics* (Studia Graeca et Latina Gothoburgensla XX; Göteborg: Acta Universitatis Gothoburgensis, 1967), 440–44.

7. L. Fine, "Recitation of *Mishnah* as a Vehicle for Mystical Inspiration: A Contemplative Technique Taught by Hayyim Vital," *Revue des Études Juives* 141 (1982), 183–90.

8. A. Stahl, "Qeriyah Pulḥanit shel Sefer ha-Zohar," *Pe ʿamim* 5 (1980), 77–86.

9. See I. Rabinowitz, ed. and trans., *The Book of the Honeycomb's Flow. Sepher Nopeth Ṣuphim*, by Judah Messer Leon (Ithaca, NY: Cornell University Press, 1983), 142–45.

10. See *Sha ʿarei ʾOrah*, ed. with introduction by J. Ben-Shlomo (Jerusalem: Mosad Bialik, 1970), I. 195f.

11. Ms. Milano-Ambrosianna, 62 fol. 113v; published and discussed by M. Idel, "Tephisat ha-Torah be-Siphrut ha-Heikhalot ve-Gilguleha be-Kabbala," *Jerusalem Studies in Jewish Thought* 1 (1981), 62–64. Cf. also *Midrash Konen*, in Jellenik's *Beth Midrash*, II. 23; the idea is already indicated in *Tanḥuma, Vayelekh*, 2.

12. G. Scholem, *On the Kabbalah and Its Symbolism* (New York: Schocken Books, 1965), 76. An old exemplary use of Gen. 36:22, in connection with rewards for the commandments, occurs in *Sifre Deut., Ha ʾazinu, pisqa* 336.

13. Moses Mendelssohn, *Gesammelte Schriften*, ed. G. B. Mendelssohn (Leipzig, 1844), v. 505.

14. *Schriften*, ed. with introduction by T. W. Adorno (Frankfurt-on-Main: Suhrkamp, 1955), I. 146.

4. Israel and the "Mothers"

1. J. Wilson, *The Intellectual Adventure of Ancient Man* (Chicago: University of Chicago, 1946), 62–63.

2. Translations of these texts may be found in J. Pritchard, *Ancient Near Eastern Texts* (Princeton: Princeton University Press, 1955), 3–4, 60–72, 129–42. A Canaanite theogonic tradition is embedded in the eighth-century B.C.E. Aramaic Sefire inscriptions (I.A. 8–12), see ibid., Supplement Vol., 1969, p. 659.

3. *The Eternal Present*, vol. II, *The Beginning of Architecture* (2 vols.; New York: Pantheon, 1964), 31.

4. Cf. the Code of Hammurapi xxvb 95ff. ("I am Hammurapi . . . to whom Shamash has bestowed truths"); and the Inscription of Yahdun-Lim of Mari, in *Syria* 32 (1955), 4 (lines 1ff.).

5. Cf. M. Eliade, *Patterns in Comparative Religion* (Cleveland and New York: Meridian, 1963), 315.

6. *Jerusalem and Athens: Some Preliminary Reflections* (City College Papers, 6; New York: City College, 1967), 8–9.

7. Apart from the oft-cited Mesopotamian parallels, the similarity between the mythic anthropomorphism in the *Egyptian Wisdom of Meri-Ka-Re* and Gen. 1 is more remarkable. Cf. Pritchard (ibid., 417); A. Volten, "Zwei altägyptische politische Schriften," *Analecta Aegyptiaca* IV, 1945, 73ff.; and S. Hermann, "Die Naturlehre des Schöpfungsberichtes," *Theologishe Literaturzeitung* 86 (1961), 413–24.

8. *Religion in Essence and Manifestation* (2 vols., New York: Harper & Row, 1963), I, 178.

9. See F. Cross, *Canaanite Myth and Hebrew Epic* (Cambridge, Mass.: Harvard University Press, 1973), 73f. The bull was undoubtedly the pedestal of the imageless YHWH, but it is a short step from there to a perception of it as a *numen* transfigured by his immanent "power." On the question of aniconism in Phoenicia, see S. Moscati, "Iconismo e aniconisme neele piu antiche stele Puniche," *Oriens Antiquus* 8 (1969), 59–67.

10. M. Aberbach and L. Smolar, "Aaron, Jeroboam and the Golden Calves," *Journal of Biblical Literature* 86 (1967), 129–40.

11. See the discussion of R. de Vaux, "The prophets of Baal on Mount Carmel," in his *The Bible and the Ancient Near East* (Garden City, NY: Doubleday, 1971), 238–51.

12. For the typological links with Moses and a thorough "tradition-history" analysis, see R. Carlson, "Elie à l'Horeb," *Vetus Testamentum* 19 (1969), 413–39.

13. See A. Deem, "The Goddess Anath and Some Biblical Hebrew Cruces" *Journal of Semitic Studies* 23 (1978), 25–30.

14. See J. Pritchard, *Palestinian Figurines in Relation to Certain Goddesses Known Through Literature* (New Haven: American Oriental Society, 1943; Krauss reprint, 1967).

15. Among moderns, W. Zimmerli accepts the veracity of Ezek. 8 in his *Ezekiel* (Hermeneia; Philadelphia: Fortress, 1979), 236–46; M. Greenberg (in his prolegomenon to the 1970 Ktav reprint of C. C. Torrey's *Pseudo-Ezekiel and the Original Prophecy*, pp. 22ff.) distinguishes between authentic reports of unofficial syncretism and inauthentic reports (projections of Manasseh's sins) of an official pagan cult. His argument has been contested (see n. 17, below).

16. Compare the remarkable prayer to Helios in the third-century C.E. magical

text called *Sepher Ha-Razim* where, however, this deity has exalted angelic status and no more; see the discussion of M. Margolioth, *Sepher Ha-Razim* (Jerusalem: Yediot Aharonot, 1966), 12–14 (Hebrew).

17. M. Smith, "The Veracity of Ezekiel, the Sins of Manasseh, and Jer. 44. 18," *Zeitschrift für die alttestamentlische Wissenschafft* 87 (1975), 11–16, has argued for a continuous royal-official cult to the Queen of Heaven.

18. For this oath, see B. Porten, *Archives from Elephantine* (Berkeley and Los Angeles: University of California, 1968), 154–55 and Appendix III. The Egyptian counterpart to Aramaic *malkat shemayin* (Queen of Heaven) is *nbt pt* (Lady of Heaven), an epithet applied to ʿAnat on a jar of Prince Psammetichus; see B. Grdseldoff, *Les débuts du culte de Rechef en Egypte* (Cairo: 1942), 28ff.

19. A basic description of throne mysticism in early Judaism can be found in G. Scholem, *Major Trends in Jewish Mysticism* (New York: Schocken p.b., 1961), 40–79.

20. *Eine Mithrasliturgie* (Leipzig and Berlin: Stuttgart-Tübner, 1966; reprint of 1923), 92–212. The Greek terms used are *teleisthai* (to be initiated or perfected and *teleutan* (dying).

21. This synopsis follows Sallustius' *De diis et mundo,* IV; see the edition and translation by A. D. Nock, *Concerning the Gods and the Universe* (London: Cambridge University, 1926), 6–9.

22. On the various aspects of the kabbala just alluded to, see G. Scholem, *On the Kabbala and Its Symbolism* (New York: Schocken, 1965), chapters 2–4.

5. From Scribalism to Rabbinism

1. See the second, enlarged English version of *Vie des Formes* (New York: G. Wittenborn, Inc., 1948).

2. See *Vom Ursprung und Zeil der Geschichte* (Muenchen: Piper Verlag, 1949), 15–106.

3. On this, cf. the valuable symposium, "Wisdom, Revelation, and Doubt: Perspectives on the First Millenium," B. Schwartz, ed., *Daedalus,* Spring, 1975.

4. See Chapter 4; first published in *The Other Side of God,* P. Berger, ed. (Garden City, NY: Doubleday, 1981), 28–47.

5. See my discussion in *Biblical Interpretation in Ancient Israel* (Oxford: The Clarendon Press, 1985), 107–09, 245, 263–65 (hereinafter *BIAI*).

6. For other post-exilic uses of *mebin* to designate skill in a levitical craft, cf. 1 Chron. 15:22, 25:7; and for the use of *hiskil* to denote knowledge and instruction by levitical personnel, cf. 1 Chron. 28:19.

7. See B. Gertner, "Midrashim in the New Testament," *Journal of Semitic Studies* 7 (1962), 276, and *BIAI,* 334 n. 50.

8. *BIAI,* 539f.

9. See *b. Hagiga* 13a and *Genesis Rabba* VIII.2, as well as the minor variations of the lemma cited.

10. Cf. *BIAI,* 487–495.

11. In these instances, *dabar* bears the sense of 'interpretation' or 'explication.' A similar, though generally unrecognized example of this sense is found in connection with the dreams of Joseph (see Gen. 37:8, and especially v. 10).

12. See my "Ha-'Ot Ba-Miqra," *Shenaton: An Annual for Biblical and Near Eastern Studies* 1 (1975), 224 n. 28.

13. Cf. 2 Kings 17:7–17 (esp. v. 13); Jer. 24:1–7 (esp. v. 4); Neh. 9:29f.

14. See S. Jafet, *Emunot Ve-De'ot Be-Sepher Divrei Ha-Yamim* (Jerusalem: Mosad Bialik, 1977), 152–58; and *BIAI*, 388–92, 401–03.

15. For a thoughtful reevaluation of this passage, see J. G. Janzen, "Habakkuk 2:2–4 in the Light of Recent Philological Advances," *Harvard Theological Review* 73 (1980), 53–78.

16. *1 Q Hodayot* I.21, following the edition of the Qumran Hymns by J. Licht, *Megillat Ha-Hodayot* (Jerusalem: Mosad Bialik, 1957). An echo of Ps. 119:18 is further suggested by *1 Q Hodayot* VIII.19: "[ho]w could I behold (*abit*) [such things] if You did not unveil my eye (*galita 'eniy*)"; and cf. the *Rule Scroll* (XI.3): "and my eye has beheld the wonders of it (*ube-niple'otav habitah 'eniy.*"

17. The mishnah is cited according to Ms. Kaufmann. Its principal differences from the printed versions is a variation in the idiom used to denote the public embarrassment of a fellow scholar (*haver*) and its position in the text: in the expression "good deeds" instead of "Torah (i.e., the merit of study) and good deeds"; and the absence of the phrase "against the halakha" (on which, see n. 18).

18. The phrase is missing in Mss. Kaufmann and Cambridge, as well as the parallel discussion in *Avot de-Rabbi Nathan*, Version A, chap. 26.

19. Cf. the discussion of E. Urbach, *Hazal. Pirkei Emunot Ve-De'ot* (Jerusalem: The Magnes Press, 1969), 265f; p. 265 n. 39 for earlier literature and explanations.

20. Cf. *BIAI*, 524 and n. 33.

21. See Josephus, *Antt.* xviii. 4. 1; xx. 5. 1; 8. 10; *Bell. Jud.* ii. 13. 4; 13. 5; vi. 5. 3. Sometimes Josephus himself assumes a prophetic persona; cf. *Bell. Jud.* iii. 8. 9; iv. 10. 7.

22. Cf. N. Glatzer, "A Study of the Talmudic Interpretation of Prophecy," *The Review of Religion* (1946), 116, 136.

23. On the one hand, the association between *mehoqqeq* and the verb *haqaq* may have called attention to the exegetical potential of this passage in terms of teaching and legislation. At the same time, there is an old exegetical tradition, already reflected in the Greek translation of the Hebrew *mehoqqeq* (staff) as *grammateus* (scribe). This interpretation is the basis for the long paraphrastic comments in the Targumim to Num. 21: 18. Ongelos, for example, glosses the noun with *saphraya* (scribes); and in the Fragmentary Targum (Ms. Paris) this gloss is further explicated by the remark that these "*saphraya* are the scribes (*saphraya*) of Israel, Moses and Aaron" (see M. Klein, *The Fragment-Targums of the Pentateuch* [Rome: Pontifical Biblical Institute, 1980], Vol. 1, 101). This paraphrase thus provides a precise rabbinic counterpoint to the Qumran tradition. Even more remarkable, in this regard, are the targumic glosses to the noun *mehoqqeq* in Deut. 33:21 (the blessing of Gad): Onqelos has "Moses, the great scribe of Israel"; while the Fragmentary Targum (*op. cit.*, 116) actually reads "Moses *the prophet*, scribe of Israel!" In this remarkable formulation, the two functions are integrated.

24. A striking parallel to these two *Hodayot* texts is found in Ben Sirah's famous 'Praise of Wisdom' (Eccles. 24). On the one hand, there is a direct comparison of the rivers of paradise to the wisdom of Torah (24:23–28). Following this, the speaker attests to his own transformation by this knowledge: "I also became as a stream from a river . . . [So] I said [thought] 'Let me water my garden . . . ; and behold! the stream became [for me] a river, and [then] my river became an ocean'" (24:30–32). Significantly, the very line quoted earlier, in which Ben Sira says that "he will pour out wisdom like prophecy," comes *just after* the preceeding similes and testimony (24:33). The tannaitic source treated below, which derives from the class ideals of the sages, is a direct inheritor of this sensibility.

25. For related midrashic sources suggesting a nexus between mystical illumination and Torah study, see M. Idel, "Mysticism," in *Contemporary Jewish Religious Thought*, A. Cohen and P. Mendes-Flohr, eds. (New York: Charles Scribner's Sons, 1987), 644f.

26. For a consideration of the role of R. Akiva in the famous talmudic story of "four who entered Paradise" (9 *b. Ḥagiga* 14b), and its place in the wider context of early Jewish mysticism, see G. Scholem, *Jewish Gnosticism, Merkabah Mysticism, and Talmudic Tradition* (New York: Jewish Theological Seminary, 1965), ch. 3. Evidence for mystical experience (divine visions) based on textual study of the Song of Songs can be gleaned from ancient midrashic sources; see ibid. (app. D, "Mishnat Shir Ha-Shirim," by S. Lieberman), 118–26.

6. The Biblical Dialogue of Martin Buber

1. *Schriften*, I, p. 158: *lauten heisst umlauten*. The above translation follows that found in Gershom Scholem, "Martin Buber's Conception of Judaism," *On Jews and Judaism in Crisis* (New York: Schocken Books, 1976), 159. In Walter Kaufmann's translation of *I and Thou* (New York: Scribner's Sons, 1970), 166, the phrase is rendered: "to sound means to modify sound."

2. The primary rabbinic source appears as an anonymous *beraitha* in *Genesis Rabba* III.6. See the pertinent discussion of A. Altmann, "Gnostic Themes in Rabbinic Cosmology," in *Essays in Honor of the Very Rev. Dr. J. H. Hertz*, ed. I. Epstein et al. (London, 1942), 28–32.

3. *Die jüdische Bewegung* (Berlin: Judischer Verlag, 1916), I, 245.

4. *Die Schrift und ihre Verdeutschung* (Berlin: Schocken Verlag, 1934), 45.

5. *On the Bible* (New York: Schocken Books, 1968), 212f.

6. Ibid.

7. Ibid., 214.

8. Ibid., 214f.

9. Ibid., 215.

10. "Der Mensch von heute und die jüdische Bibel," in *Die Schrift . . .* , 33–38. This section does not appear in the translation of the essay in *On the Bible*. Also cf. Buber's remarks on nature and Spirit in *Israel and the World* (New York: Schocken Books, 1963), 34.

11. "Herut: On Youth and Religion," *On Judaism* (New York: Schocken Books, 1967), 172.

12. Ibid.

13. *On the Bible*, 214.

14. Ibid., 215.

15. Ibid., 215.

16. See *Ha-Ru'aḥ ve-Hamitzi'ut*, "Darkhei Ha-Dat Be-Artzeinu," (Tel Aviv: Maḥbarot Lesiphrut, 1942), 118–26.

17. *Moses*, 103.

18. Ibid., 109.

19. "Biblical Leadership," *On the Bible*, 148.

20. See in *The Philosophy of Martin Buber*, The Library of Living Philosophers, P. A. Schlipp and M. Friedman, eds., (Lasalle, Ill.: Open Court, 1967), 728f.

21. "The Dialogue Between Heaven and Earth," *On Judaism*, 215f.

22. *Ha-Ru'aḥ Ve-Hametzi'ut*, 126.

23. "The Man of Today and the Jewish Bible," *On the Bible*, 6.

24. Ibid., 7.
25. "Biblical Humanism," 216.
26. Ibid.
27. Ibid.
28. See the above-cited essay (n. 1) by G. Scholem, "Martin Buber's Conception of Judaism," 166f.

7. Martin Buber's *Moses*

1. *Neue Schweitzer Rundshau*, n. f. 20.3, July. Translated in *A Believing Humanism* (New York: Simon & Schuster, 1967), 32f.
2. *Moses. The Revelation and the Covenant* (New York: Harper & Row, 1958), 7.
3. See the discussion ibid., 15f.
4. See "Gedanken über Mythos, Epos und Geschichte," *Kleinere Schriften*, IV, 74 (originally in *Deutsches Museum*, III, 1813, 53).
5. *Good and Evil* (New York: Charles Scribner's Sons, 1952), 53.
6. See *On Judaism* (New York: Schocken Books, 1967), 172.
7. *Op. cit.*, 36.
8. *On the Bible* (New York: Schocken Books, 1968), 172–87.
9. *Moses*, 10.
10. See the recollections of H. Rauschning, "A Conversation with Hitler," *The Ten Commandments. Ten Short Novels of Hitler's War Against the Moral Code*, A. L. Robinson, ed. (New York: Simon & Schuster, 1944), xiii.
11. *Good and Evil*, 6.

8. Speech and Scripture

1. Following N. Glatzer, *Franz Rosenzweig: His Life and Thought* (New York: Schocken Books, 1953), 257f. (hereinafter: *FRLT*); cf. "Die Schrift und Luther," *Kleinere Schriften* (Berlin: Schocken Verlag, 1937), 154 (hereinafter *KS*).
2. Unless otherwise indicated, translations follow *The Star of Redemption*, trans. William W. Hallo (New York: Holt, Rinehart and Winston, 1970), 1 (hereinafter: *Star*). The original text of *Der Stern Der Erlösung* (hereinafter: *Stern*) is cited from the 2nd edition (Frankfurt am Main: J. Kaufmann Verlag, 1930).
3. This reference to death's "poisonous sting" at the beginning of the *Star*, and the accompanying references to death as being "swallowed up . . . into the eternal triumph" (pp. 4–5), reveal Rosenzweig's profound exegetical imagination and technique from the outset. For while the first citation derives from Hos. 13:14, and the second from Isa. 25:8, they are cited together in Paul's sermon in 1 Cor. 15:54f. That this latter is Rosenzweig's "base text" is further proved by the fact that his allusion to these prophetic passages follows Paul's Greek version (and not that of the received Hebrew or Septuagint versions). On the other hand, the phrase "eternal triumph" combines the Hebrew 'forever' and the Greek 'victory,' and may even borrow from rabbinical midrash (where the word *neṣaḥ*, 'forever,' is often taken as *niṣaḥon*, 'ultimate victory'). Rosenzweig uses these citations as a kind of leitmotif throughout the *Star*, as we shall see. The rhetorical power of their use here is twofold. First, Rosenzweig has abstract philosophy cite biblical Scriptures—thereby injecting a dialectical negation of pure thought into thought's claims from the outset (since biblical Scriptures are, for Rosenzweig, the paradig-

matic expression of the priority of speech and concrete living over a priori reason). Second, Paul cites these verses in order to demonstrate the triumph of Christ over the death which derives from sin and the Law. However, in this opening part of the *Star,* the fact of death defeats the thoughts of philosophy; while in the last two books, the relationship of Judaism to Christianity, as well as the link between the Law and "eternal life" are thoroughly reenvisioned.

4. Rosenzweig plays with this dialectic in various ways. Cf., for example, his statement that this claim of "Nought" is "not Nought, but something (*Das Nichts ist nicht Nichts, es ist Etwas*)"; *Stern,* I. 9f.

5. This core element of Rosenzweig's thought was influenced profoundly by Eugen Rosenstock and the latter's *Angewandte Seelenkunde.* Rosenzweig read this work in manuscript "a full year and a half before [he] began to write" the *Star;* cf. the acknowledgement in "The New Thinking," *FRLT,* 200. On speech as ensoulment, see below, n. 11.

6. On defiance (*Trotz*), cf. *Star,* 67f, 167f. Note too the remarkable statement (*Star,* 170): "[There is] . . . no faithfulness without defiance."

7. *Star,* 176; *Stern,* II. 112f. Rosenzweig thus sees Gen. 22:1 as the completion or fulfillment of Gen. 2:9. Rosenzweig was particularly drawn to Abraham's response, and discusses its significance again in his *Jehuda Halevi* (Berlin: Verlag Lambert Schneider, n.d.), 196 (*ad* 55). Martin Buber was also drawn to these two texts; cf. *Between Man and Man* (New York: Macmillan, 1965), 166, and his extended "teaching" in *The Way of Man* (Secaucus, NJ: The Citadel Press, 1966), 9–14.

8. *Stern,* II. 113. This readiness is also expressed as a "pure obedience, all ears (*reiner Gehorsam, ganz Ohr*)"; ibid., II. 113f. By this gloss, Rosenzweig says the readiness is an attentive hearing—thus giving great importance to the echo of the verb 'to hear' (*hören*) in the noun 'obedience' (*Gehorsam*). Also cf. his phrase 'attentive hearing' (*ge-horsame Hören*), II. 114, and the discussion on *KS,* 154 below.

9. *Stern,* II. 115. Rosenzweig also speaks of the "wholly pure language of love" (*ganz reine Sprache der Liebe*) (*Star,* 177; *Stern,* II. 114) and the "imperative of love" (*Star,* 178; *Stern,* II. 116).

10. In *Star,* 188, Rosenzweig speaks of revelation as establishing a "midpoint and beginning in one." Also cf. his diary entry of 2.5.22, in *Franz Rosenzweig. Der Mensch Und Sein Werk: Gesammelte Schriften I, Briefe und Tagebücher,* ed. Rachel Rosenzweig and Edith Rosenzweig-Scheinmann, with Bernhard Casper (Haag: M. Nijhoff, 1979), 2. Band (1918–29), no. 740, 778 (hereinafter: *GS I.2*).

11. Given the positive uses of the noun *Erlebnis* in *Star,* especially in contexts discussing revelation and love (cf. *Stern,* II. 122, 124, 143), one can hardly doubt that Rosenzweig missed the echo of these words. By contrast, Buber had polemical misgivings about this type of experience. See the important discussion by P. Mendes-Flohr, *From Kulturmystik to Dialogue: An Inquiry into the Formation of Martin Buber's Philosophy of I and Thou* (Ph.D. diss., Brandeis University, 1973).

12. Cf. his remark that "revelation . . . endows the mute self with speech and soul at once" (*Star,* 198; *Stern,* II. 142), and that "[u]nder the love of God, the mute self came of age as eloquent soul" (*Star,* 198; better: 'speaking soul' for *redenden Seele, Stern,* II. 143). Rosenzweig suggests a profound relationship between the speaking self and the harmony of music, which latter is the result of the "inspiring" (or: 'ensouling,' *Beseelung*) of "mute" details though "pitch" (or: 'voice,' *Stimmung*).

13. Rosenzweig speaks of a "pure present," a *reine Gegenwart;* cf. *Stern,* II. 115.

14. Rosenzweig also speaks in this regard of *unmittelbaren Gegenwärtigkeit* (*Stern*, II. 115), "immediate presentness" of the command of the moment.

15. This time is of the pure present, repeatedly called a "Today" by Rosenzweig (cf. *Heute*, in *Stern*, II. 115, 128). His use of this word to signal the response to the voice of revelation in the "here and now" is an allusion to Ps. 95:7 ("this day if you would hear My voice") as interpreted in the Talmud (*b. Sanhedrin* 98a), where *hayyom* (this day; today) is the potential day of redemption *if* you hear (viz. heed) the divine Voice. The 'Now' of revelation thus proleptically anticipates and simultaneously participates in the structure of redemption—a time within, yet ultimately beyond temporality (for though Rosenzweig concedes that the true present gives birth to the awareness of past and future, his assertion is that the moment itself is without temporal awareness).

16. *Star*, 202.

17. Ibid., 201.

18. Alluding to the opening words of Genesis 1 ("In the beginning" and "God created"), which he translates and presents at the beginning of Book II as "*Im Anfang*" and "*Gott schuf*" (and also "*Der Anfang ist: Gott schuf*"; "The beginning is: God created"; *Stern*, II. 1), Rosenzweig says at the beginning of Book I, "*Im Anfang ist das Ja* (In the beginning is the Yea)" and "*Das Ja ist der Anfang* (Yea is the beginning)." He also says that the archetypal word 'Yea' is "the 'sic!' the 'Amen' behind every word" (*Star*, 27).

19. See *Stern*, II. 87; *Star*, 155. The allusion is to the midrashic comment of Rabbi Meir in *Genesis Rabba* IX. 5. Meir was presumably enabled to find scriptural support for his (somewhat gnostical?) position on the basis of a dialectical variant (*mavet ≈ mawt*). A similar midrash on the word *me'od* (in Lam. 5:22) can be found in *Exodus Rabba* XXXI. 10.

20. I.e., in the exegetical traditions of rabbinic midrash.

21. 'And' is the third of three archetypal words for Rosenzweig, not equal to 'Yea' and 'Nay' "in originality, for it presupposes both, yet for the first time helps both to a vital reality." At the same time, the word " '[a]nd' is the secret companion not of the individual word but of the verbal context. It is the keystone of the arch of the substructure over which the edifice of the *logos* of linguistic sense is erected" (*Star*, 33).

22. Cf. *Star*, 153. "It is to cognition what the "good!" is to volition . . ." Biblical texts dealing with light recur as a midrashic leitmotif throughout the *Star* (e.g., Ps. 36:10, pp. 253, 295; 89:16, 157, 424).

23. *Star*, 219; another allusion to Isa. 25:8.

24. The original *miy yitten* of Song of Sol. 8:1, which is translated as "O that you were" but more literally glossed as "who would grant," functions as an important grammatical moment for Rosenzweig—expressing the transition from the initial glimmer of love (in revelation) to the hope for its eternity (in redemption). Cf. *Star*, 203, and the similar use of the *miy yitten* of Job 14:13, in connection with the prayer for the kingdom (the phrase is rendered by "Oh [sic!] that you would" and "who would grant that"). Rosenzweig refers to the *miy yitten* of Num. 11:29 as Moses' "messianic wish." See *GS I.2* (diary entry for 27.4.22), 777.

25. *Stern*, II. 150.

26. Cf. the remarks in *Star*, 236.

27. See "Das neue Denken," *KS*, 377–98 (supplementary notes to the *Star*).

28. Cf. *Star*, 250.

29. Ibid., 250f.

30. There are several thematic links between Psalm 115 and other texts used in *Star* which are particularly worth noting here. First, there is the issue of the 'muteness' of the idols who are not bearers of love through revelation. For those who trust in them, there is thus no overcoming of death, but rather a descending into the pit of death, *dumah*—a word punningly related to a similar word for silence (viz, 'speechlessness'). Finally, just as the recipient of divine love can love and praise, the worshipper of mute idols is "like them"—mute. The simile particle (here: *kemo-*) recalls and must be understood in relation to the other 'like' constructions: "strong *as* (*ka-*) death"; "*like* (*ke-*) a brother"; "*as* (*ka-*) a seal"; "love your neighbor *as* (*kamo-*) yourself" (or in Rosenzweig's understanding: "for he is *like* yourself"). This particle thus functions as a thematic element of sorts, producing diverse dynamics of content and form.

31. *Star*, 253.

32. Ibid.

33. Cf. the section title at *Star*, 294, and the comments following on mathematical symbols and grammatical forms.

34. While there are many biblical passages which recur throughout *Star*, and give its teaching a midrashic dimension, it bears particular mention that the cluster of verses in Song of Songs 8 has a special thematic power—and one might even say that the *Star* is, in some respects, a philosophical midrash on these verses. Note, for example: 8:1 ("would that you were like a brother"; "I would kiss you"); 8:2 ("I would kiss you"; cf. 1:2, and its many variations in the book); 8:4 ("do not awaken . . . love until it break forth"; alluded to in *Star*, 274f. in connection with premature arousal of the divine kingdom, just the way the verse is used in classical midrash; cf. *Song of Songs Rabba* II. 1. 7); 8:6a ("set me as a seal," cf. *Star*, 204, 381, 395 and *b. Shabbat* 55a; "for love is as strong as death"); 8:6b ("divine fire"; cf. the title of III.1, "The Fire or the Eternal Life"); 8:10 ("as one who finds peace"; cf. *Star*, 185, 303, 253).

35. *Star*, 198. The expression "eloquent soul" translates *redenden Seele* (better: "speaking soul"); cf. nn. 6, 11. The phrase "presentness of our experience" (in revelation) translates "*der Gegenwärtigkeit unseres Erlebnisses*"; *Stern*, II. 143. Cf. nn. 8, 10.

36. *Star*, 199. In a remarkable midrashic reworking of Isa. 55:8 (p. 151), Rosenzweig even says: "The ways of God are different from the ways of man, but the word of God and the word of man are the same. What man hears in his heart as his own human speech is the very word which comes out of God's mouth." In "Die Schrift" (*KS*, 136), he says that God's word requires a human word, and cannot do without it.

37. *b. Ḥagiga* 3b.

38. Cf. "Das Formgeheimnis der biblischen Erzählungen," *KS*, 180.

39. This is the talmudic formula implied by the expression *hors daraus* in "Neuhebräisch?" *KS*, 226 (cf. Glatzer, *FRLT*, 270). Elsewhere, Rosenzweig formulates this "command of the hour" as "to open my ears" (*FRLT*, 246; *GS I.2*, 1004).

40. Among other reasons, according to Rosenzweig, Scripture lacks aesthetic "distance" (*die ferne*); cf. "Die Schrift und das Wort," *KS*, 135.

41. "Formgeheimnis," *KS*, 180.

42. Cf. ibid., 173, where Rosenzweig mentions *Stichwort und Pointe*.

43. For this example, see ibid., 174f.

44. In "Die Schrift und das Wort" (*KS*, 135) Rosenzweig speaks of the holy spirit as human speech. Cf. H. Cohen, "Heilige Geist," *Jüdische Schriften* (Berlin, 1924), III, 176ff.

45. See in Glatzer, *FRLT*, 258, 235f. and 246, respectively.

46. Glatzer, ibid., 236; "Die Bauleute," *KS*, 108f.

47. Glatzer, ibid., 258.

48. Rosenzweig uses this dictum at several points in *Star* (pp. 250, 406). He also refers to the first part of the dictum ("turn it [viz. Scripture] and turn it again" when he says that the "Jew always thinks . . . to turn his legal doctrines (*Gesetzeslehre*) this way and that (*um und um zu wenden*); sooner or later it would turn out to have 'everything in it' (*alles darin*)." See *Star*, 406; *Stern*, III. 188.

49. Glatzer, *FRLT*, 246; *GS I.2*, 1002 ("*Aber man vernimmt anders, wenn man im tun vernimmt*").

50. Cf. Glatzer, ibid., 206.

51. *Star*, 290.

52. Cf. Glatzer, ibid., 206.

53. *Stern*, I. 8; *Star*, 4. Also: "*Er soll bleiben.*"

54. *Stern*, III. 201; *Star*, 416.

55. Ibid. A midrashic dynamic is apparently at play here: an allusion to Ps. 16:5 and to God as one's 'portion' and 'part' (*ḥeleq*); and an allusion to the rabbinic use of *ḥeleq* as being one's 'portion' in the World to Come (cf. *M. Sanhedrin* X.1). Thus: to partake fully of one's portion, at any hour, would mean to participate in eternity in the here and now.

56. Mic. 6:8. The particle *mah* (what) functions as a *Leitwort* in this prophetic discourse (v. 3, twice; v. 5, twice; v. 6), grammatically establishing the rhetorical and forensic ground of the whole (along with other question forms)—all of which set up the more assertive use of the particle in v. 8 (twice) and the declarative *kiy 'im* ('but'; cf. the uses of *kiy*, 'for') in vv. 2–3.

57. *Stern*, III. 211; *Star*, 424.

58. *Stern*, III. 202; *Star*, 417.

59. Cf. *Star*, 170: "[T]he attribute of faithfulness endows the soul with the strength to live permanently in the love of God." Through this "affirmation and constancy" the soul breaks beyond "the moment" of human love and "hears an 'unto eternity' in itself which is no self-delusion." Now "[t]he soul is at peace in the love of God, . . . and now it can reach beyond 'the uttermost parts of the sea' and to the portals of the grave—and is yet even with Him" (p. 171). This last phrase ("*und ist doch immer bei Ihm*" *Stern*, II. 108), recalls Ps. 73:29 ("And I am always with You" *va'aniy tamid 'imakh*). The citation of this text in this context (of spiritual steadfastness) is all the more poignant insofar as this very verse was chosen by Rosenzweig for his tombstone (diary entry for 9.6.22); *GS I.2*, no. 770, 793.

9. The Teacher and the Hermeneutical Task

1. From *The Collected Dialogues of Plato*, ed. E. Hamilton and H. Cairns; trans. R. Hackforth (Bollingen Series 71; Princeton: Princeton University Press, 1964).

2. Rabbinic Judaism speaks of two separate but complementary Torahs: the oral Torah and the written Torah. See W. Bacher, *Die älteste Terminologie der jüdischen Schriftauslegung* (Leipzig, 1899), I, 89, 197. For a wide-ranging discussion, see E. E. Urbach, *The Sages* (Cambridge: Harvard University Press, 1987), Ch. 12.

3. For a recent discussion, see M. D. Herr, "Continuum in the Chain of Transmission," *Zion* 44 (1979), 43–56 (Hebrew).

4. Ibid.

5. See the illuminating comments of S. Rawidowicz, "On Interpretation," *Proceedings of the American Academy of Jewish Research* 26 (1957), 83–126.

6. For a different attempt, see N. Frye, "Levels of Meaning in Literature," *Kenyon Review* 12 (1950), 246–62.

7. See the discussion and historical evaluation in G. Scholem, *On the Kabbalah and Its Symbolism* (New York: Schocken Books, 1965), ch. 2.

8. This is what P. Wheelwright, *The Burning Fountain: A Study in the Language of Symbolism* (Indiana: Indiana University Press, 1959), 3–4, 55ff., called "steno-language." For other aspects of literal language, see the comments of O. Barfield, "The Meaning of the Word 'literal,'" in L. C. Knights and B. Cottle, eds., *Metaphor and Symbol* (London, 1960), esp. 48–57.

9. See *Sifra* on Lev. 13:47.

10. See A. Einstein, "Augenmusik im Madrigal," *Zeitschrift der internationalen Musikgesellschaft* 14 (1912), 8–21.

11. For the distinction between the extrinsic and intrinsic approach to literature, see R. Wellek and A. Warren, *Theory of Literature* (London, 3rd. ed.; 1963), pts. 3–4.

12. Cf. ibid., pt. 4, where the category of intrinsic literary study is discussed. For a different use of these categories, see F. W. Bateson, "The Function of Criticism at the Present Time," *Essays in Criticism* 3 (1953), 1–27.

13. This is the notion of explication, which has been defined as "the examination of a work of literature for a knowledge of each part, for the relation of these parts to each other, and for their relation to the whole." See G. Arms and J. M. Kuntz, *Poetry Explication* (New York, 1950), 20.

14. Cf. his "Leitwortstil in der Erzählung des Pentateuchs," *Die Schrift und ihre Verdeutschung* (Berlin: Schocken Verlag, 1936), 284–99.

15. For this and other structures, see my discussions in *Text and Texture: Close Readings of Selected Biblical Texts* (New York: Schocken Books, 1979).

16. For biblical examples, see Exodus 3, Jeremiah 1, and Ezekiel 1–3.

17. Cf. N. Frye's remarks in "The Knowledge of Good and Evil," *The Morality of Scholarship*, ed. M. Black (Ithaca: Cornell University Press, 1967), 3–28. He observes that whereas detachment is moral in an intellectual context, it is a vice in a social one (p. 9). My point is that study is always social—in the interpersonal and cultural sense.

Conclusion: The Notion of a Sacred Text

1. See above, ch. 9, n. 2.

2. *M. Yadayim* III.2; and the discussion in S. Leiman, *The Canonization of Hebrew Scriptures* (Hamden, CT: Archon Books, 1976), 102–120.

3. This expression (*aiyn muqdam u-me'uḥar ba-Torah*) is a hermeneutical principle of the school of R. Ishmael; cf. *Mekhilta de-Rabbi Ishmael, Beshalaḥ* 7 (beginning, in re Exod. 15:8).

4. The tannaitic expression, *dibrah Torah ki-leshon benei adam* ("The Torah speaks in the manner of human speech") appears as a rule of R. Ishmael (vs. R. Akiva) concerning the meaning of verbal repetitions in the same sentence; see *Sifra Numbers* (on 15:31). From the time of Judah ibn Qureish (9–10c) this idiom was used regarding scriptural anthropomorphisms (see W. Bacher, *Die Bibelexegese der Jüdischen Mittelalters vor Maimuni*, 1892, 72).

5. See the discussion of this and related texts in ch. 3.

6. See the discussion of G. Scholem, *On the Kabbalah and Its Symbolism* (New York: Schocken Books, 1965), 50–65.

7. *Shi'ur Qomah* (Warsaw, 1883), 85d.

8. See Scholem, *op. cit.*, 37–44.

9. Cf. above.

10. *Semiotikè: Recherches pour une sémanalyse* (Paris: Seuil, 1969), 146.

11. *Structuralist Poetics* (Ithaca, NY: Cornell University Press, 1975), 139f.

12. Abraham is called an *Ivri*, or 'Hebrew', in Gen. 14:13; and already the Septuagint translates it with the sense of "crossing over" an area (i.e., "Abraham the Over-crosser"). However, my midrash here was rather inspired by a teaching of Rabbi Nahman Bratzlaver (*Liqqutei MoHaRaN*, no. 65.d, end) which says that God is called "the God of the *Ivrim*" (Exod. 3:18) because Israel (the *Ivrim*, Hebrews) transcends (*'overim*) through faith all rationality that pretends to know God in the void created by His apparent absence from the world. Only faith, he says, can assert God's presence where it cannot be known.

13. See the discussions in E. Becker, *Escape from Evil* (New York: The Free Press, 1975), 4, 64, 69–71.

14. Ibid., 144.

15. *Mekhilta de-Rabbi Ishmael, Bahodesh*, 5 (middle, on Exod. 20:2).

INDEX